7011

Library
Oakland S.U.M.

THE LION AND THE LAMB

Paradoxes of the Christian Faith

THE LION
and
THE LAMB

PARADOXES OF THE CHRISTIAN FAITH

by

GERALD KENNEDY

ABINGDON-COKESBURY PRESS
NEW YORK ● NASHVILLE

THE LION AND THE LAMB

COPYRIGHT MCML
BY PIERCE AND SMITH

All rights in this book are reserved. No part of the text may be reproduced in any form without written permission of the publishers, except brief quotations used in connection with reviews in magazines or newspapers.

Scripture quotations, unless otherwise designated, are from the American Standard Version, copyright renewal 1929 by the International Council of Religious Education.

SET UP, PRINTED, AND BOUND BY THE PARTHENON PRESS, AT NASHVILLE, TENNESSEE, UNITED STATES OF AMERICA

This is for
GRACE and RAY

PREFACE

IT HAS GROWN ON ME WITH EACH YEAR OF MY MINISTRY THAT WE modern preachers have to find the point of our preaching again. What are we to be, commentators or witnesses, philosophers or apostles? What is the unique function of the Christian pulpit? What themes are we to proclaim? Our preaching has gone wrong not simply because of our technique, although that can stand improvement. The fault is more serious. It is a loss of authority because we are not sure what the "good news" is for such a day as this. We have lost the burden of a unique, divine, saving Word.

The dialectical theologians have been right when they sought to bring the Church back to a sense of the supernatural element in Christianity. They have been wrong when they raised an impenetrable barrier between God and man. In their attempt to dig us out of the pit of humanism they have sometimes cast us into the prison of human helplessness. They have had a true understanding of the modern world's oversimplifications. But the answer is not a complete rejection of common sense and human reason, nor a denial of the presence of God in ordinary affairs.

What we need is to get back to the personal nature of Christianity. Once we keep this in mind, we know that there is the necessity of being found by God, and that there is created by that divine-human encounter a tension. The gospel sees truth in personal terms, which means there is in it a large element of paradox. It knows that human virtues are not absolutes, and that when they go unchallenged by the tension of an opposite virtue, they go wrong.

One of those wonderful experiences that set a man's imagination aglow came to me some years ago when I read G. K. Chesterton's chapter on "The Paradoxes of Christianity" in his fine volume Orthodoxy. No man could write about paradox with such grace and effectiveness as Chesterton. He made the point—

and it is still convincing to me—that heresy is always the attempt to narrow and overemphasize one side of the gospel. He insisted that orthodoxy feels the pull of the opposites, but keeps them from flying apart, and thus keeps them true.

Maude Royden in an article on "Pagan Virtues and Christian Graces" said that when the Sermon on the Mount recommends humility, for example, it presupposes self-respect, and that "every Christian grace was founded upon the rock of honor and loyalty, courage and justice, a piercing vision, a great strength. It is only the strong who can really be gentle."

And so, for better or for worse, I have tried to follow some of the implications which such ideas have suggested. Increasingly I am convinced that the strict logic of a philosophy is its weakness, and the courage to proclaim saving paradoxes is Christianity's strength.

The substance of some of these chapters was delivered in somewhat different organization as the Peyton Lectures on Preaching in February, 1949, at the Perkins School of Theology. To the gracious invitation of Dean Eugene B. Hawk to deliver these lectures I am indebted for the stimulus to set down my thinking on this subject that has resulted in this book.

GERALD KENNEDY

CONTENTS

9

CONTENTS

11

I

LOGIC AND LIFE

I thank thee, O Father, Lord of heaven and earth, that thou didst hide these things from the wise and understanding, and didst reveal them unto babes.   —Luke 10:21

MEN HAVE SELDOM BEEN MORE CONCERNED TO FIND A WORKABLE way of life than they are now. The book which claims to tell people how to live happily can be sure of a sale. The lecturer with a magic formula for making life interesting will have an audience. We are almost desperate in our desire to have someone tell us how to live in the midst of tension. The truth of Thoreau's remark that most men live lives of quiet desperation was never more obvious.

This is a sure sign of the sickness of our time. Whenever a generation talks long and anxiously about a philosophy of life, you may be sure it does not have one that works. We are not worried about our health until we are sick; we are not concerned about happiness except when we are bored; we are not anxious for the good life until we are overwhelmed with the evil of our present life.

Our search is limited and confined by our scientific presuppositions. We think that all of our problems can be reduced to an equation. If two parts of hydrogen and one part of oxygen equal water, then happiness ought to equal two parts of this and one part of that. We go to the counselor in the same spirit we go to the druggist—we want a prescription. We cannot believe that any value is beyond our external manipulations. We are like the two Arabs Colonel Lawrence took with him to London. They were entranced by the gadgets of Western civilization. When they were leaving, Lawrence asked them what they would like for a gift. They said they wanted two hot water faucets. They assumed that by turning the handle they might have hot water in the middle of the desert, the same as in a London hotel room. We are like that. Tell us how to turn a handle or mix a tonic. Give us an intellectual proposition. In a word, let some wise man formulate for us a philosophy of life.

Desire for a Philosophy

Youth is the time for philosophizing with assurance, for youth is not aware of its own limitations and the limitations of human knowledge. With what confidence we participated in bull sessions when we were in high school and college! How profound and unanswerable were our opinions in those midnight fraternity or sorority debates! None of us would give up the memories of those memorable occasions, but the older we grow, the more we realize that there are more things in life than we dreamed about in our discussions. Is it too much to say that the most we can hope for from a philosophy is a formulation of the right questions? In a realm of intangibles, in a realm beyond logic, are the answers.

A book written by an eminent physicist proposes a next step in the development of man.[1] The author says that we need to discover a "unitary method of thought." Quite so! But how? Around what center shall the unity be established? He apparently assumes that if men are told about this need, they will find an answer to it. It is still the scientific heresy that knowledge is moral.

We go wrong in all of this because we assume that men are purely rational creatures who act only from rational motives. We think that the healing of the ills of our life is an intellectual matter. It is not. We think we go wrong because we are ignorant. We believe that if we had facts enough, we would be able to chart our course realistically. Not so! It is not true that a man's happi-

[1] Lancelot Law Whyte, *The Next Development in Man* (New York: Henry Holt & Co., 1948).

14

ness depends on his knowledge. For character is not all of a piece, and the most incongruous traits exist side by side.

Some time ago a group of workmen were putting up a pre-fabricated house in Illinois. In an attempt to make some kind of record, they put it together so fast that one of them was caught in it. They had to tear down a section in order to let him out. Which is a parable! The philosophical system imprisons the human spirit. Systems are always needing to be torn down to let out the soul of man.

The Inadequacies of Philosophy

Because the rational side of a man's life is one of the essential things about him, philosophies will always be needed, for each man is and must be to some extent a philosopher. But the truth is always beyond, and each philosophy is partial. No one knows this better than the student who has to study a history of thought. Each great thinker had an idea that was true. But there is the constant necessity of balancing one man's thought with another's; we must put this system over against that one. There seems to be something that is uncapturable by thought, and that indefinable something finally wrecks the system.

What does this mean? It means that it is not a matter of the world's being either reasonable or unreasonable. It is rather, as G. K. Chesterton pointed out, that the world is almost reasonable, but not quite. There is meaning in life. It has a purpose. There are principles underlying the world, and a mighty order is discernible. But there is also a kind of wildness which lies in wait for the logician. There is a kind of defiance of our reason which is also a part of life. There is the unexpected, the unreasonable, the terribly mysterious element which waits in ambush for our unwary minds. There is, in a word, something in life which hates logic and will not be confined by it.

Let us learn a lesson from precious stones. Sometimes their beauty is due to their imperfections and their irregularities. It is a trace of foreign matter that catches the eye. The chance presence of chromium in a piece of beryl makes that stone an emerald, and star sapphires contain tiny impurities which reflect light. One of the main problems in the manufacture of synthetic stones is how to copy nature's imperfections. A cold perfection is lifeless.

Francis Bacon was aware of the danger of assuming more order in the universe than there actually is. This man, who stood at the threshold of the modern period and was able to perceive the limitations of the medieval scholastics, saw that in the enthusiasm of discovering "laws" of nature we might fail to see the areas beyond the laws. It is this warning which we have failed to heed. The unfriendliness of science toward revelation and miracle has been due to its cocksureness that although absolute order cannot be proved, it must be assumed. Science has given us a closed universe—with a vengeance. Nothing in life, says our logic, should be assumed beyond the realm of rational description and explanation. Perhaps nothing in modern times has been more damaging to true wisdom and progress than this dogma.

When a philosopher has established his system, he can hardly help believing it is a finality. Now everything must fit the system. The fact which seems to contradict his order he interprets in such a way that it falls into the right groove. Or if something in life seems to defy even this treatment, he assumes that it is too unimportant to warrant serious consideration. The trouble is that systems of thought tend to become strait jackets or Procrustean beds. Philosophers are affected by this tendency, as well as ordinary men. The preconceived orderly system has the same dangers as prejudice. No man can write history or interpret history without having his own preconceptions color his interpretation of the facts. There is no such thing as a purely objective history, nor can there be. But, at the very least, we should demand that historians refrain from converting history into world systems.

Making history fit a system is like having made up one's mind about another person. Once one has accepted a judgment about another man, he should no longer expect to know him. Each

16

person is full of surprises. There are no set rules that will encompass a personality satisfactorily. If a man has made up his mind that another race is lazy, for example, there is nothing members of that race can do to change his mind. He will interpret every action in terms of the laziness thesis. The philosopher with a system is always doing that to life. Indeed, he cannot escape doing it. The system misses something, overemphasizes something, and disregards something. It has an unredeemed lust for order and consistency.

But not only that. A philosophy is to an amazing extent determined by a man's temperament. It rises from many causes. It is colored by personal relations, by health, by glands, by too many stimulations, or by too few hours of quietness. What appears to one man as the good life may appear to another as a nightmare. The optimist cannot help viewing life differently from the pessimist, and his interpretation may seem like drivel to the pessimist. Every philosophy, being a human affair, has to be confronted with the question of what person it is to be applied to and when and where.

My idea of a wonderful way to spend an evening is to stay home and read a book. I'd rather do that than almost anything I know. But to lay down as a general principle that the way to spend one's evening is to stay home and read a book would cause a vast number of young people, especially, to turn away in disgust. Stay at home every night? That is the last thing they want to do. So any philosophy is necessarily a limited thing and, to a large extent, dependent on the temperament of the philosopher.

An editor broke away from Communism and went back into the Roman Catholic Church. He wrote a book confessing his guilt and giving the reasons for his conversion.[2] It is not such a long way as you might think from an authoritarian system like Communism to an authoritarian system like Catholicism. But the interesting thing about the book is the man's analysis of why

[2] Louis Francis Budenz, *This Is My Story* (New York: Whittlesey House, 1947).

he sinned against the light for so long. He says that, although critical of the Communist Party in America, he continued in it because he was enslaved by the Marxist "philosophy." It was his yardstick by which he measured all policies, and no matter what happened, he always had a system which could explain the most contradictory facts with a forced unity. Thus he went on as if he had been mesmerized.

When we are seeking for life, we need more than an intellectual pattern. We must always be on guard lest our philosophy keep us from life.

Life Is Paradox

The inadequacy of philosophy is due to the fact that life is paradoxical. That is, it demands that we hold together in a kind of tension what seem to be contradictions. This is not to say that life is an absolute dualism, though it may appear both dualistic and monistic at the same time. Its unity is over and above its diversity. The desire for logic will never allow this to be recognized. But the Christianity which is truly realistic is not afraid of paradox and sets forth its truth in paradoxes. The Christian stumbling block for many men is its insistence that if we are to find life, we must be willing to lose it.

Man himself is a paradox. He is a free spirit, and he makes his own choices. In his mind he roams the heavens, and in his spirit he becomes a citizen of eternity. No external force can conquer him, and all external authorities finally have to yield before his ability to say No. But man is also determined by physical laws, and his body is severely limited by his physical environment. He cannot spread his arms and fly or live under the sea like a fish. If he leaps from a high building, he gets hurt. It seems that he must be continually at war with himself. He wants to be free, but he is a slave. How can a free spirit imprisoned in a physical body find a way of life that is not a constant conflict? Of one thing we can be sure—it will have to be a way beyond logic.

The Freudians need criticism at many points, but Freud—like

Paul—was one of the great pioneers in helping us to understand human nature. One of his observations was the positive desire for life which he called "libido" and the negative impulse toward death which he called "mortido." A man, he suggested, wants life and he wants death; he says Yes and he says No. Neither of these impulses can be eliminated. They must somehow find their rightful places in an over-all synthesis. For it is true, in a way which our philosophies can never quite explain, that for a man to find life he must not be afraid of death.

Even physics, which is in some ways a most static science, tells us that the most stable objects seem to be balances of forces. The physical universe is not at all what we once thought it was. The so-called solid stuff is not solid. What we once thought was stationary mass is really whirling energy. Electrons may be particles or they may be waves, and the physicist has to use an equation that will work in either case. At the very heart of things there seems to be an uncertainty. You might call it chance, or perhaps you might suggest that the physical universe has a kind of free will. Apparently our picture of the world as a machine is no longer a fitting one. The universe is more like an idea, and it seems to have less and less the likeness of a closed system. Even here, then, the wildness lies in wait. Things are not so solid and safe as we thought.

In our social behavior and our ethical systems we can never reduce things to rules. Here too there has to be the tension of opposites. Once we try to make absolutes out of ethical principles, we turn our virtues into vices. Take mercy as an example. Is it a good thing for a man to bestow mercy? Certainly! It "droppeth as the gentle rain from heaven." But suppose mercy is not checked by justice? Why, then mercy becomes a sentimental, mushy thing that makes human relationships impossible. Over against our willingness to be merciful, there has to be our insistence on justice. Somehow these two qualities have to be kept in balance.

Gentleness is a Christian virtue. But it is an austere kind of gentleness, which to some minds is illogical and therefore impossible. It has been the great accomplishment of the gospel to hold our understanding of the gentleness of God's commands over against the severity of his purposes. Men must do the same thing in their personal relations. Christian graces must rest on ethical virtues. No single virtue can stand alone.

Or consider humility and pride. Certain it is that Christians are warned against the sin of pride and urged to practice the virtue of humility. The theologians who warn us against pride as the most unlovely of human weaknesses and the fundamental sin are right. But a humility that is not challenged by a sense of worth and a feeling of self-respect becomes a crawling thing which no one can admire. If humility knows no anger and lacks the power of an inner confidence, it is not at all admirable. Men should be humble, and they should also have a holy pride in the value of their sonship. All of this is in the realm of spiritual mystery and goes far beyond our intellectual power to describe. We know when we see a person with these combinations in the right proportion, but we do not know how to write out the formula for them.

There is a verse in Isaiah describing the future society under the rule of God: "The wolf also shall dwell with the lamb, and the leopard shall lie down with the kid; and the calf and the young lion and the fatling together; and a little child shall lead them." (Isa. 11:6.) We can easily miss an important point in this prophecy. It does not say that all shall become the same. The wolf is not to become lamblike nor the calf lionlike. Each maintains his own nature, but they dwell together. Let the leopard remain a leopard and the calf keep the qualities of a calf. But let them walk together and find their unity in the leadership of a little child.

Something of that is necessary in all of life. Things as different as the lion and the lamb must be held together in subjection to a higher power. There must be a divine discipline which can keep each from destroying, or being destroyed by, the other. This takes more than a set of rules or principles. It takes the power of God and a divine revelation.

The Gospel Above Logic

Christianity suggests a way of living that often seems contrary to logic. It is not something you could have guessed. It is not something reducible to reason. It breaks in. It startles. It overwhelms our carefulness. It opens a vista so breath-taking that we can hardly stretch our minds and spirits wide enough to take it in. The man who has not allowed his familiarity with it to breed contempt knows that this is the most exciting thing he has ever heard. If the gospel is true, what a devastating thing it is to our intellectual limitations.

Chesterton once remarked that a mathematician tries to get the heavens into his head, while the poet tries to get his head into the heavens. This is also the difference between a philosopher and a religious man. The philosopher tends to say that if it cannot be crammed into his head, he does not want it. The religious man knows that the mystery of life is too vast to be crammed into anything, especially his head. He must therefore open his heart and his mind to God, who alone can give him light. Let him find faith.

This is why our religion goes wrong when it falls too much under the sway of systematic theologians. Theology is not an intellectual exercise of the cloister, but a statement of experience from Christians facing live issues. When Christianity is regarded as a "system" contained in certain intellectual propositions, the life goes from it and its truth is distorted. For then it moves toward a "philosophy of religion" which is mummified religion. This is not to minimize the importance of theology's contribution to Christianity, but it is to warn against substituting philosophy for faith. Forms are necessary, but they are not to be confused with life. If one seeks the heart of the gospel, he must not search for it in the creeds or in the carefully reasoned discourses of the scholastics. He must meet the one who said, "I came that they may have life."

How often the gospel goes against all our common sense. It says that if we want to get, we must give. How can a man get by giving? Let him get by keeping, says the mind. Keep the other fellows out and protect your investment; never share with the outsiders. This is the reasonable way. But the gospel says that if we follow that way, we shall lose even the little we have. The path to abundant living, says our Lord, is by way of renunciation. Albert Schweitzer found that after he had given up his music and his scholarship for the sake of his missionary task in Africa, it all came back to him sevenfold. The time came when he was lecturing at the great universities and playing the organ in all the leading capitals. What a mysterious thing this giving is! What a denial of logic life is! In order to get, you must give.

Or let us consider the matter of winning. Do you want to win? Everyone does. Well then, says Christianity, do not be afraid of losing, for to gain the world you must lose. But if you determine to win the world at any price, you will discover that you have lost your own soul, for which a man can give nothing in exchange. How often the careful man has planned his career in terms of what he wants only to find his deepest desires have been denied and what he really wanted has been lost. Yet how often a man has been called upon to give up what his ambition told him was valuable, only to find that a better gift was given in its place.

A man has to die to live. He must be born again. He has to think of himself as unimportant in order to be important. To heal himself he must forget himself and heal others. The kind of religion which turns men's eyes inward upon themselves is false and destructive. There is a heretical, watered-down, unbalanced religion, which is very popular today. It massages the emotions and makes people so aware of themselves that we are in danger of becoming a generation of college freshmen with one semester of abnormal psychology. Jesus called men to follow him, knowing that they would be healed by forgetting themselves in his service. We save our lives by risking them.

Christianity dares to go beyond logic, because life does. It dares to say the thing that seems to contradict reason, because life does. It is not afraid to state its truth in paradoxes, because life does. To

22

men as they stand at the crossroads it comes, not with a system, but with a revelation. It demands a plunge, a decision, an action. For this is where the issues of life are decided, and not in an armchair working intellectual exercises.

The Christian can never quite say what the gospel means. But he knows that while others stand by the roadside debating and wondering, he is a part of a mighty fellowship which knows an answer. He sees others debating what constitutes the good life and the happy life. But all of his energies have been drawn into a great crusade which—as Paul said—makes his life a constant pageant. If the Christian spoke to these debaters, he could use the words Henry IV addressed to the tardy Crillon: "Hang yourself, brave Crillon: we have fought at Arques and you were not there." But his spirit is more like that of his Lord, who wept over the city because it was too proud and sophisticated to accept his gift of life. Christians have found life and truth in a realm beyond logic.

II

WAY AND POWER

I am the way.   —John 14:6

For I am not ashamed of the gospel: for it is the power of God.
—Rom. 1:16

It is important to remember that the early Christians were
not called philosophers. They did not take their place in the ancient
world as another school alongside the sophists, the stoics, or the
skeptics. They were not a debating society, nor were they an academic discussion club. They were called "Followers of the Way."
Which is to say they were not concerned primarily with abstract
problems. They were recruits in a war or members of a caravan.
Philosophers are interested in studying the map and perfecting it.
Christians have heard a trumpet call.

Not only that, but Christians of the first century were not after
order primarily. Remember the incident in Thessalonica after Paul
had preached in the synagogue. The Jews stirred up trouble by
announcing that "these that have turned the world upside down
are come hither also." (Acts 17:6.) Their chief concern was not
the *status quo* but the Kingdom of God. Followers of a way never
quite know where it will lead, and they go forth without any certainty of what will be required of them.

One of the greatest insights in the New Testament was the word
in the Fourth Gospel, "I am the way." (John 14:6.) You do not
say that about men—even great men. You say that a man has character, or ability, or vision. You do not say, "He is all I need to know

24

about life." But that is what Christians say about Jesus. They mean that he does not give them merely a philosophy. They mean that in him there is the clue of life and the light to live by.

A SERIOUS MIND

Yet we are aware that many men never find Jesus as the Way. Why? Primarily because they are not willing to approach him with the right attitude of mind. We cannot find the Way unless we approach Jesus with a serious mind. We must have some sense of what is at stake. If he is truth, then it is a matter of life and death that we find him. The issues of eternity hang in the balance.

Too many people approach Jesus with a flippant attitude. They are not as concerned with him as they are with the question of what they will wear to a party. Religion too often assumes the same importance as deciding what political organization to join. People want to philosophize about it, but they do not want to consider seriously the gospel's demand for a decision. They never assume that they will actually do anything about it until some more convenient season.

The eighteenth century liked to talk. One of the arts most appreciated was that of conversation. In some ways its representative man was Dr. Samuel Johnson, who enjoyed folding his legs and having his talk out. Too many religious leaders regarded good talk more highly than right conduct. But Wesley did not regard philosophical speculation of first importance. He was always on the move seeking to enlist someone for Christ. His field of activity was more a thing of the mine, the market, and the long road than it was of the study or drawing room. He could never forget what a serious business Christianity is, because it was for him a way.

It is not only the young and the unlearned who take a flippant attitude toward Christ. Such is too often the response of the intellectuals. First-rate scientists have made statements about Christianity which would be appropriate only in the mouth of a ten-year-old child. They reveal the same lack of perspective and knowledge. One of the heaviest crosses Christians have to bear is listening to the inane, ignorant, and yet disdainful remarks made about Christianity by people who have not taken the time to learn what they are talking about. Let us make no mistake about this: the first demand which the Christian way makes upon men is that they should approach it with a mind aware of the urgency and consequences of the decision Christ asks them to make.

George Moore, the Irish writer, developed a reputation for saying shocking things. But one of his friends said that he did not kiss and tell; he told but did not kiss. This is the attitude so often of the man who speaks much about Christianity. There is no real experience behind it because there has never been a serious desire for experience. It is a sad truth that many a man who has never faced the real issues of the gospel never hesitates to talk glibly about it.

An Expectant Mind

Again, we must come to the gospel with an expectant mind. Remember the great word of Jesus in the Sermon on the Mount: "Ask, and it shall be given you; seek, and ye shall find; knock, and it shall be opened unto you: for every one that asketh receiveth; and he that seeketh findeth; and to him that knocketh it shall be opened." (Matt. 7:7-8.) Underlying all of his teaching is this emphasis on expectancy. He looks upon the complacent with unhopeful eyes, even when they possess a considerable amount of moral rectitude. But he has hope for every expectant person, no matter what his present situation may be.

If a man is to find the Way, he has to ask himself what may happen to him if the promises are true. What ought to happen in this situation? Should he meet God at this next turning? In this quiet moment should the still, small voice be speaking? Once a man has learned to listen and look with expectation, he begins to hear and see the mysteries of the Kingdom of God. Here is something about Jesus that is different from other men. John Drinkwater put it in these lines:

> Shakespeare is dust, and will not come
> To question from his Avon tomb,

And Socrates and Shelley keep
An Attic and Italian sleep.

They will not see us, nor again
Shall indignation light the brain
Where Lincoln on his woodland height
Tells out the spring and winter night.

They see not. But, O Christians, who
Throng Holborn and Fifth Avenue,
May you not meet, in spite of death,
A traveler from Nazareth? [1]

Perhaps it is this experience that makes the historical interpretation of Jesus incomplete. He is a historical figure, but he is more. He meets men now, as he did long ago, if they have the seeking spirit and possess great expectations. But without that expectancy they will pass him by, for they never see him.

A SINCERE MIND

To find the Way a man must approach it also with a sincere mind. There is a mental disease called "negativism" which makes it impossible for a man to believe anything. Every time an idea occurs to him, a hundred doubts appear. Finally he cannot act at all and must be confined in an asylum, for men cannot live without believing. The disease may not become serious enough to incapacitate a person physically, but it may keep him from ever seeking the truth.

On the other hand, there is a disease in which all discrimination has disappeared. In this case the victims believe everything. They are the people who buy widely advertised products, regardless of their qualities. They are the people who accept everything they read in the papers or hear over the radio. They have never considered that when the news sources are concentrated, it is easy to

[1] "To and Fro About the City," from *Seeds of Time* (Boston: Houghton Mifflin Co., 1927).

propagandize certain viewpoints. Thus there are these two diseases which a man must guard against. The sincere mind moves cautiously and questioningly between the two dangers. It considers a proposition until it shines in its own light. Only then can a man know, for truth has its own illumination.

A man went to see a minister one time and opened the conversation with these words: "I hear you are a modernist. I am a fundamentalist, and I want to question you." What a way to begin! Every word the minister spoke was pounced upon by the man and twisted to signify heresy. At last the minister had enough and said, "You are not here for any honorable purpose. You are here to quibble. You do not care to understand my position or to help me understand yours. You have no desire for our minds to meet. For such as you I have no time to waste." It is this insincere attitude which characterizes so many approaches to Jesus.

AN ADVENTUROUS MIND

Also, a man must come to Jesus with an adventurous mind. I know a lady who developed a phobia of germs. She has read too many articles about how these little rascals wait to pounce upon us and make us sick. For her the world is full of millions of microbes all united in a plot to destroy her. Eating at a restaurant is an ordeal. She assumes the glass is covered with bacteria and the food full of poison. She wipes everything off carefully, but she still looks at the food suspiciously. Her home is full of gargles and antiseptics. She will not use the telephone until she has disinfected it.

What is wrong with this? Only that fear has triumphed over faith. Of course life is dangerous, but healthy people take it in their stride. The frightened die a hundred deaths, and the brave die but once. Yet how many people approach other matters besides health with this timidity. The Way will never be undertaken by them. For as the Bible points out so clearly, the religious life is a pilgrimage beset with many dangers, and only the adventurous will follow it.

There are two choices which confront us as we face life. Ultimately we have to decide which is of paramount importance—to avoid error or to risk the pursuit of truth. It is the choice between doubt and faith. If we decide in favor of the first proposition, then life will be a matter of escaping error. That means we will prefer the negative kind of life, for action of any kind makes a man's life vulnerable. Any enterprise may lead us astray. Any act of believing entails the risk of mistaking falsehood for truth. If the main purpose of living is to keep our life unspotted by mistakes, then we will withdraw to some sanctuary where our life will be spotless but sterile.

On the other hand, suppose we decide that the pursuit of truth is the most important thing. Then we will gladly take the risk of making wrong decisions and temporarily believing half-truths in order to move in the direction of the Way. No man can live this adventurous life without occasionally being misled. No doubt there will be times when the careful man will be able to say, and probably will say, "I told you so." There will be moments of despair when one confesses himself to have been duped. Quite so! But these are the necessary risks of the game and will be taken gladly by the man who believes that to draw closer to the truth is more important than to be untouched by error.

Rudyard Kipling wrote a poem entitled "The Explorer." A man goes to the frontier and is persuaded to stop. Yet he feels the call of something out beyond the mountains. Finally he leaves his security behind him and goes out alone. More dead than alive, he finally gets through a mountain pass and finds a rich new empire. Others follow him and develop the new land. Farms and cities are established. Then at the end of the poem, the explorer thinks about the whole experience, and he says:

> Yes, your "Never-Never country"—yes, your "edge of cultivation"
>   And "no sense in going further"—till I crossed the range to see.
> God forgive me! No, I didn't. It's God's present to our nation.
>   Anybody might have found it but—His Whisper came to Me! [2]

[2] From *The Five Nations*, copyright 1903, 1931 by Rudyard Kipling. Reprinted by permission of Mrs. George Bambridge and Doubleday & Co.

That is the call of the gospel as a way. It demands that we approach it with a serious mind, an expectant mind, a sincere mind, and, most important of all, an adventurous mind.

POWER

Now the other main thing to be said here is that the gospel is also power. Once again it differs from philosophy. It does not say that this is an intelligent way to live, but from here on it is up to you. It says, "But ye shall receive power, when the Holy Spirit is come upon you." (Acts 1:8.) It is this promise that men overlook, and as a consequence they hesitate to accept it as their way. They do not know that, though it is beset with difficulties, it provides the power to deal with the difficulties. Paul found this to be true, and he writes: "For I am not ashamed of the gospel: for it is the power of God unto salvation to every one that believeth; to the Jew first, and also to the Greek." (Rom. 1:16.) That was the favorite text of one of my friends, because he said it was the most marvelous discovery a Christian made.

Those who are familiar with the history of our Western exploration and development know there was produced during that period a species known as "mountain men." They had come from Eastern farms and villages. Some of them had been merchants, and some were missionaries. At least one of them was an English nobleman. But whatever they had been previously, after they learned to live in the midst of danger and cope with the vast distances and the high places, they became "mountain men." It was a title of distinction and honor, because it could not be given; it had to be earned. Something of that kind happens to Christians. They are men who have been given power and adequacy. No matter who they were previously, they are now followers of the Way. They are not afraid. They are not boasters. They have a quiet confidence that comes to men who have overcome the world. Paul is their prototype. Says he, "I can do all things in him that strengtheneth me." (Phil. 4:13.)

CONSISTENCY

The gospel has the power of a consistent, total view. When we follow it, everything makes sense. It is too bad that so many people have only fragmentary ideas about Christianity. They think it has something to do with Sunday and the worship hour only. It is all right for children, and they feel that probably a few years in Sunday school will not hurt the youngsters. It may even have a use when men get old and tired and the fever of life is over. But in the meantime they keep it on the periphery of experience. Ralph Sockman once said that people treat the Christian faith as sentimental maidens treat a wedding cake—they break off a little piece of it and put it under their pillows to sleep on. The lack of a consistent point of view is one of the dangers of our time. Our tragedy is that the thing which could fill the need is often disjointed and broken into fragments. We dissipate the power of the gospel by our refusal to accept it completely.

We make a great mistake in assuming that Christians are called upon to build the Kingdom of God. This has been the humanistic heresy, and it has caused much grief. We have thought we were called to create a new order by sheer determination and will. But that is not so. The Kingdom of God is. It is the way things are. We do not build it; we enter it. We become citizens of God's government. To us there is given the vision of reality, and beyond the conflicting parts we find unity. Now there comes the glimmer of a perfect whole. Faith leads us where we have not yet traveled, and beyond our limited experience we are aware of an eternal order.

This gives power to life. If we know at least there is a mighty plan which centers around God's concern for men, we can be at ease. It is the fear that there is nothing above all the fragments that weakens human effort and is destroying our civilization. Wholeness is power, for it sets the great questions in their proper setting. What seems to be at opposite poles suddenly becomes all of a piece. The psalmist wrote:

31

He healeth the broken in heart,
And bindeth up their wounds.
He counteth the number of the stars;
He calleth them all by their names.
(Ps. 147:3-4.)

This experience gives a man dignity and assurance. He is no longer a pigmy in the midst of a hostile environment. He is a part of a consistent universe, created and maintained by God, who is the Father of men.

CONFIDENCE

For another thing, the gospel releases the power of confidence. This is the great need in our time. We are under the direction of too many frightened men. They do not have the confidence of a great tradition or the assurance of a way of life to which they are committed. They are scared, and scared men cause most of the trouble in the world. For when men make their decisions under the control of fright, those decisions are usually wrong.

We in America are a tragic example of this. With more strength and potential power than any other nation, we ought to be leading the world in the direction of security. The masses who watch us going down the beaten track of war, which is always the track of beaten men, look to us in vain for some hopeful sign. Our policy seems to be one of going from this crisis to the next. Instead of going forward, we go backward. Suddenly we are told that tomorrow about three o'clock we will be attacked. The next day it is hinted that all our navy is gone and we have no airplanes left.

In the midst of all this confusion the military urges us to follow the paths of the old world. In our hysteria we hear a thousand voices saying that the only answer is the answer of militarism, which has never worked for anyone. If we cannot prove that a new way would lead us where we want to go, we know that the old way cannot. It is a time for Christian prophets to rise in the great tradition of the prophets of Israel. We need voices to warn us that there is no safety in alliances and war material. Let the Church say to

32

these hysterical politicians: "Woe to them that go down to Egypt for help, and rely on horses, and trust in chariots because they are many, and in horsemen because they are very strong, but they look not unto the Holy One of Israel, neither seek Jehovah!" (Isa. 31:1.)

What each man needs in his own personal life is the confidence that comes to men who have found the Way. The panic-stricken man reveals he knows not the Way. Energy that might be used in constructive effort is wasted in worry. It is not a rational fear of a real danger. It is present when things go right as well as when they go wrong. If business is good, the anxious man is sure it is better than it ought to be, and that means an even greater disaster in the future. There is a disease of the mind and spirit that is like cancer in the body. All orderly control is gone, and a wild, lawless fear has its destructive way. The disease is not cured by taking thought, but by experiencing the love of God.

The followers of the Way have found the power of confidence in a presence that is with them always, "even unto the end of the world." These men do not belong to any single class or condition. They are rich, they are poor; they are young, they are old; they are famous, they are nameless; they are brilliant, they are simple. But in the midst of peril and panic their courage and calm remain unbroken. It is as if they are stimulated by a contact with someone who has convinced them he has everything under his control. Shakespeare had a phrase for it in *Henry V*: "A little touch of Harry in the night." For the Christian it is a little touch of Christ. Ah, that's it! If only we could bring into our world that calm, we would find a way out. How desperately do we need this power of confidence which Christ brings to Christians!

High Purpose

Finally, the gospel brings the power of a high purpose. Tennyson wrote in "Sir Galahad":

> My good blade carves the casques of men,
> My tough lance thrusteth sure,

My strength is as the strength of ten,
Because my heart is pure.

It has been fashionable to regard those lines as sentimental. Perhaps there is revealed in them a certain moral pride, but they express a great truth. There is strength in the pure heart and the clean purpose. Strength is unloosed within us when our motives are right, and this is one of the sources of the gospel's power.

Let us not forget Britain in the dark days of 1940 and 1941. In some ways that was her greatest hour. There was no reason to expect she would hold out and risk total annihilation. But Churchill reminded the English that until the Nazis had conquered their Island, they could never win. Englishmen stood as the final barrier to the conquest of democracy. The knowledge of that issue made them mighty, and their strength was as the strength of ten. It is better that a nation should have a high purpose than that it should have a huge armament.

The most weakening thing a man can have in his life is a secret knowledge of his own selfishness and meanness. He may make all the excuses he wishes, but if in his own heart he knows he is engaged in an enterprise that is cheap and degrading, his strength ebbs away. His chief enemy is his own conscience. No matter how strong and ruthless he appears, he is weak. But if he has given his life to something good, there is a hidden source of power which carries him through the bad times. Nothing so ennobles and fortifies a man as a good purpose. The life committed to Christ always feels welling up within it the assurance that it is undergirded by the power of God.

The Christian gospel demands an unconditional commitment. If it does not have that, its promises are void. Many a man waits to learn if a rich man is going to follow the Way. Will the socially elite follow it? Is it acceptable to those prominent people? Our redemption begins when we see the irrelevance of such questions. All we need to know is that when any man sees the gospel as the Way and follows it, he finds released into his life God's power.

34

III

SIN AND GRACE

But where sin abounded, grace did abound more exceedingly.
—Rom. 5:21

ANY MAN WHO WEEK AFTER WEEK TRIES TO PROCLAIM THE CHRISTIAN interpretation of life and truth knows that he can be used as a witness against himself. Last Sunday's sermon can be quoted against this Sunday's. But even Paul was not beyond this, and he too can be quoted against himself if ideas are taken out of their context. This is inevitable and due to the paradoxical element in reality.

There is no better example of this seeming inconsistency than Christianity's doctrine of sin and grace. No point of view is more aware of the blackness of sin and the tragedy of evil. Over against the easygoing philosophy which assumes that men are good the gospel proclaims the depravity of the heart. Where some insist there are people just doing things which are neither good nor bad, our religion describes the uncrossable gap between sin and virtue. Since the coming of Jesus men have been more aware of the corruption in their souls than they ever were before.

Yet on the other hand, Christianity announces that for the poison of sin God has provided an antidote in the grace of his Son. Just when we think that our faith is to be regarded as the most somber view, it breaks out with a million flashing lights of hope and assurance. The gospel ordained that the Christian was to be more aware of evil than any other man and also more aware of God's grace which could deal with evil. In this, as in so many things, Paul puts

35

it best, and we learn that wherever sin abounds, grace abounds more exceedingly.

Something Has Gone Wrong

Christianity begins with the assumption that something has gone wrong in human nature. The Old Testament portrays that truth in legend and story, and the New Testament reveals it in the Cross. Our fathers spoke of total depravity, an almost unmentionable phrase in our day. Our squeamishness in this regard is hard to understand. We have grown accustomed to advertisements saying horrid things about otherwise lovely and dainty young ladies. Through our realistic writers we have become familiar with the most brutal revelations of human perversion. But in the realm of theology we maintain a priggishness that would shame the Victorian era.

What did Christian theologians mean by their doctrine of depravity? Did they mean that everything in man's nature is completely evil? I think not. They meant that even the good things in human life can go wrong and often do go wrong. They meant that there is a great chasm between what God has a right to expect us to be and what we actually are. No man can consider seriously a single day in his life without observing how good intentions produce bad results. One who has taught a Sunday school class of small boys cannot doubt the reality of original sin.

Our modern viewpoint is quite different. Take our attitude toward juvenile delinquency as an example. No one can deny that broken homes, slum sections, inferiority complexes, and handicaps cause many a youngster to get into trouble. On the basis of this, the social worker's philosophy seems to be that no one is to blame for anything, at least until he is twenty-one years old. One of the fundamental dictums of this outlook is: "There is no such thing as a bad boy." If that is true, then things have changed during the past few years, for I was a boy once, and I was often a bad boy. Long before the law held me accountable, I made choices for which I never doubted my responsibility, and they were often bad choices. Of all the silly, sentimental teaching which has ever characterized any generation the denial of human badness is one of the worst.

36

Because we begin with a false premise, we suggest false answers. The cure-all for delinquency is to be more playgrounds, though it has been pointed out that some of the worst gangs of the big cities organize on the public playgrounds. We preach our doctrine of no-accountability so that any youngster whose environment is not all that it should be already has the perfect alibi for anything he wants to do. The conclusion seems to be that until there are no broken homes, no drunken parents, and no handicapped lives, no one is responsible.

Against this idea the gospel will set its face like flint. It will not be so impressed with outward actions as this other philosophy, but it will deny that evil is caused by outward circumstances alone. It will insist on the necessity of a power not ourselves working a miracle within as the answer to the situation. To improve the environment is paramount, but even a perfect environment will not cure the gone-wrongness in human nature.

None of us will have any difficulty in believing that something has gone wrong with our enemies. That something is wrong with the Communists is so plain that it needs no argument. Certainly something has gone wrong with the man who is suing us in the courts. That neighbor who is so quarrelsome illustrates the proposition clearly enough. But that we too are a part of that universal sin is not so easy to believe. Yet there are no exceptions. "All we like sheep have gone astray." (Isa. 53:6.) Until every nation, every class, and every man is willing to include himself in the gone-wrongness of the world, there is no salvation.

Two men were walking in the country when they discovered a beautiful flower. As one man bent over to pick it, a snake came from under its leaves and slithered away. The man drew back startled, and his companion remarked, "Is the snake more real than the flower?" [1] To that question we must answer that one is as real as the other. There is the flower, but there is also the serpent who so often lies in wait within the shadow of the flower. Sin is a universal reality.

[1] Lynn Harold Hough, *Adventures in the Minds of Men* (New York: Abingdon Press, 1927), pp. 87-88.

To Be Saved from Ourselves

Now most men are aware of our need for salvation. Few men are content with life as it is for very long. In this "time of troubles" there is an almost universal longing for a better world. But our tragedy is in seeking it from the wrong source. We cannot believe that what we need to be saved from is ourselves.

We believe too often that all we need is to be saved from a few bad men in the world. In a desperate attempt to whip up some enthusiasm for the last war we were told that at last we knew our real enemy, and this time we would have a war to end all war. It was pointed out that twenty-five years ago we fought Germany but did not keep her defeated. Now it had to be done again. Since the same people had caused the same trouble twice in a generation, we now knew what we had to do. Well, we sent the Germans down into the most complete defeat a modern nation has ever known. We can keep them there. The bad men have been killed, and still we are not saved. Then comes the crowning illusion of them all. We are told that we made the mistake of thinking the bad men were in Germany instead of in Russia. How long, O Lord, how long will we go on believing that salvation is a matter of killing a few bad men or slaughtering a few more millions of "the enemy"?

Still another group comes along to tell us we can be saved if we make everybody afraid of us. This group, usually associated with the first, believes that if we have enough atom bombs, the biggest navy, and enough men under arms, we are safe. But this is a tried way that has never succeeded. If history says anything plainly, it says that when men become afraid, they get desperate and they do mad things. Then comes the destruction which engulfs everyone and brings down the strong and weak together.

Some tell us that the whole thing is a problem to be solved by materialism. We are told that a few billions strategically placed will bribe others to be our friends. So far as our domestic situation is concerned we are advised to provide enough bread and entertainment to keep everybody numb and happy. As long as there are enough taverns with enough television sets in them, there is nothing much to worry about. These people assume with a kind of blithe innocence that loneliness and despair are to be anesthetized with pleasure.

In all of this we cannot be made to see the inadequacy of our own wisdom. If science can prepare us for war, why can it not prepare us for peace? We are still under the sway of the belief that God is not essential. He may have his place, but we are sure we know best. When it comes to salvation, we will trust our wisdom. We will save ourselves, and it seems quite beyond us to comprehend that it is our own selves we need to be saved from.

In all of this we receive much advice and we give much advice. A poetess tells us that "just the art of being kind" is all we need to learn. Precisely, but, dear lady, that is just the art we do not know how to learn. It is our unkindness and our cruelty that is the problem which we do not know how to solve. Be unselfish, we are commanded. Ah, if we only could! But our ego is stronger than our good desires. We do not need to be convinced that if all the world were unselfish, our troubles would be over. But where is the voice to explain how this is to be done? Be just, we are advised. Again, we will not argue the advantages of justice. But when it comes to being just, we are as helpless as when it comes to being unselfish. We can admire it as an ideal, and we can speak eloquently about all of these virtues in the abstract. But to find a way to realize these qualities in our own poor lives is not so easy.

No man can think profoundly about the human situation without coming to the unpleasant conclusion that he is the greatest obstacle which stands in the way of better things. Remember Victor Hugo's story *Ninety-Three*? A ship is caught in a terrific storm, and when it is at its height, the frightened crew hear a terrible crashing sound below. They know what it is. A cannon they are carrying has broken loose and is crashing into the ship's sides with every smashing blow of the sea. Two men at the risk of their lives manage to fasten it again, for they know that it is more dangerous than the storm. And that is like human life! It is not the storm which is our greatest danger. It is that terrible corruption loose within us which will send us to the bottom. Until we can be saved from that, there is no hope for us. Some power has to help keep safe and sane the wild enemy within.

God Has Done Something About It

If we had to stop with this universal experience, we would be of all men the most miserable. For we Christians are more sensitive to this dark reality than others. But precisely because we are Christians we have the answer, which is that God has done something about sin. He did it in Jesus Christ.

This seems to be the clue to the meaning of Jesus. We have been through a time when liberal thinkers have tried to keep Christianity vital with the assumption that its founder was a good man. This, they assumed, was all we needed to believe. That idea has run its course and stands revealed in all its inadequacy. I have known many good men, and so have you. But there was never the slightest hope that they could save us from our sins. The experience of Jesus has always been something vastly different from giving admiration to a man who set us a good example. It has been something vastly different from loving one who died for high ideals.

The meaning of Jesus is nothing less than an act of God entering into the human situation to redeem it. He was a new power breaking into the world's tragedy. He was God's concern for his children manifesting itself with might and tenderness. We may express it in different ways, but back of all our fumbling words there is the assurance that Jesus Christ was God's proclamation that he would redeem the gone-wrongness in human life.

This is the difference between an ethical system and our religion. Whenever we lose sight of the truth that our God has sent his Son to us that we might have life, we have betrayed the gospel. The sign of the reality of our Christianity is in its saving power. Whenever Christianity loses its ability to save men from their sins, it has lost its life. All the emphasis on its successful and rich enterprises is only a pitiful attempt to cover its real failure. There are enough such enterprises in our world already. The Church's central task is to produce men who will testify that once they were blind but now they see.

There are those who say that believing God has done something about this salvation releases man from his responsibility. Such critics have never understood it at all. For it is not until a man has reached the end of his own powers and is ready to give up that he is able to find his redemption in God. God does not do for us what we must do for ourselves. He does for us what we learn at last we cannot do for ourselves. Strangely enough, this experience does not lessen human effort but increases it and makes it effective. For until we know and accept our limitations and dare to trust his everlasting mercy, we cannot use our own powers to their full extent.

It is too bad some Christians have assumed that God's salvation is a matter of placing them in a kind of embalmed perfection. It is a terrible thing for a man to believe he has been "anointed." There is a kind of evil religion which creates a "Messiah complex." Then a man feels he is above his brethren and beyond their right to criticize him. It is the acme of spiritual pride and passes under the pretension of being a superior spiritual experience. It is born when we try to make God's action in Christ a static experience. Let us not regard salvation as a mechanical process culminating in the raising of fixed barriers around our little souls. It is the releasing of power. It is a divine alchemy transforming our weakness into strength. It is a divine assurance that because God has acted, never again need we be the helpless victims of evil.

The Grace of the Lord Jesus Christ

As a man continues in the Christian way, great phrases describing the Christian experience come to shine in his mind with ever increasing light. One of those phrases is "the grace of the Lord Jesus Christ." It speaks of gentleness and sympathy, of tenderness and mercy. These words are a part of the Christian's special vocabulary and must needs remain meaningless to the non-Christian. They are something which "none but his loved ones know." But when our shoulders are bowed with burdens too heavy to carry, the thought of "the grace" comes to wonderfully sustain and comfort us.

Yet how difficult it is to define the meaning of "the grace of the Lord Jesus Christ." Here is something which speaks of spiritual transformations. If one has ever sat beside the bed of a person he loved so profoundly he did not think he could go on living without her, he will remember how he watched the face of the doctor for some hint of hope. Then perhaps he was summoned from the room to hear the verdict, and the doctor told him that the crisis was over and she would live. Those words are like the words of grace which come from Christ to the desperate man whose best life is nearly dead from sin.

How these words come with indefinable light and refreshment to the man who has gone into the depths of evil! He may have been possessed with a kind of madness which drove him farther into the morass in a vain attempt to deaden his remorse. Finally, in a terrible revulsion against it all, he turned and heard the promise of God's grace. Then there poured over him a cleansing stream which seemed to wash him with purity. Forever afterward he could speak of the grace of the Lord Jesus Christ only with a note of holy reverence in his voice.

Many a man has committed what seemed to him to be an unforgivable sin. He never thought it was possible for him to do such a revolting thing. But he did it. Never again, he thought, could there be any feeling of self-respect possible for him. Never again could he be sure of his own integrity. Never would he find it possible to be at peace with himself and with life. He went to bed at night with a prayer that he would not dream about what he had done. But whenever there was a quiet moment, this horror leaped upon him out of the past. Then he turned in a final desperation to God, and the terrible burden was lifted. Somehow, in a way he could never quite understand or describe, he had been freed and forgiven. It was grace which had worked the miracle. Then, like

Paul, he could say that where sin does abound, grace abounds even more.

The active love of God for sinners reaches men in Christ and creates in them a saving faith. Jesus did not talk about a doctrine, but in his actions men saw what they knew they had no right to ask for, and something they did not deserve. This experience of grace became the foundation on which they stood and the basis of their hope. It was at the center of their good news of salvation. While this emphasis is not lacking in the Old Testament, it never came with full power to cleanse and save until the Word became flesh.

The experience of God's grace involves a submission and a yielding, yet a mechanical overpowering of the human will is quite foreign to it. This is where the Catholic and Protestant conceptions part company. We cannot believe that it comes from an infallible institution or ever acts without regard to the human response. Precisely because it is personal—which is to say it is given by a Person and it is received by persons—it is free. But like love, it is both a gift and a claim. It compels because it makes no demands; it makes moral effort effective because it makes futile the concept of human merit.

Christians find themselves in the strange position of being more aware of the difficulties which stand in the way of goodness than other men. As Théodore de Bèze's *Confession of Sins* puts it, they are placed in a position of "recognizing our faults more and more." Yet they are more sure of the reality of goodness and the possibility of its achievement. They do not cover up the unlovely nor minimize their insatiable lust for evil. But they have been touched with the beauty of holiness which comes as a gift of the grace of God. You cannot understand Christians and what may seem to be their contradictions until you understand these two experiences.

When John Bradford saw a criminal being taken to execution, he said, "There but for the grace of God goes John Bradford." The moralist would say the chap was no doubt getting what he deserved. It would never enter his mind to think that he might have been in the criminal's place. Or if it did occur to him, he would glory in his own virtue and thank God he was not as other men, especially this poor criminal. But the Christian knows that he in himself is not greatly different from others. He knows that if he relied on his own powers, he would not be safe from such a fate. His character is a gift from God. Its establishment and maintenance are not due to any personal virtue but to grace.

Shortly after Gandhi's death John Haynes Holmes wrote a fine article about him. Holmes described the first time he had seen the Indian saint. It was in 1931, on a cold, foggy, rainy day at Folkestone, England. Gandhi was coming to London to attend the famous Round Table Conference. A few people waited at the pier to welcome him, and Holmes found himself talking to an English policeman, who said as he pointed up the coast, "Do you know, just round those cliffs is the place where Julius Caesar came when he invaded Britain?" Then, pointing down the coast, he said, "Only a few miles beyond that fog bank is the place where William the Conqueror landed just before the battle of Hastings." Just then the awaited ship came into sight, and Holmes said to himself, "Here comes the third and greatest conqueror of Britain." But certainly Gandhi did not look the part. He went pattering up the pier to his train in a loin cloth and a shawl. He had no armor and no sword. He was followed by a few friends, but no soldiers. Yet sixteen years later India was free.

So it is with the grace of our Lord Jesus Christ. It comes with no trumpets blowing and no outward show of force. It comes quietly and without boasting. But it comes to conquer the evil in a man's life and set him free. Against all the hosts of sin its quiet attack is more terrible than an army with banners. The gentleness of the grace is the victor over the blustering fierceness of evil.

John Newton's hymn says it in these words:

> 'Twas grace that taught my heart to fear,
> And grace my fears relieved;

How precious did that grace appear
  The hour I first believed!

Through many dangers, toils, and snares,
  I have already come;
'Tis grace hath brought me safe thus far,
  And grace will lead me home.

Or in Paul's words, "But where sin abounded, grace did abound more exceedingly."

IV

FOOLISHNESS AND WISDOM

Because the foolishness of God is wiser than men.
—I Cor. 1:25

THE APOSTLE IS SUGGESTING THAT THE GOSPEL OFTEN APPEARS TO BE foolishness, but that this apparent foolishness is a higher wisdom. He is not afraid to speak of what appears to be "the foolishness of God." He is saying that what Christianity accepts as truth often appears to the worldling as madness. The Christian, therefore, must not be afraid to hold together in tension reason and something which seems to deny reason. For out of his recognition of an unknowable comes his profoundest wisdom.

In our attitude toward reason we often go too far in one direction or another. We do it as individuals and as denominations. There are those, for example, who limit their religion to the bounds of their understanding. They put a premium on satisfactory explanations. They may not know what they believe, but they know what they do not believe. They would rather trust their careful logic, and they find it difficult to confess there is anything beyond their comprehension. Churches made up of these self-confessed intelligentsia are too often respectable but powerless. They cannot propagate themselves.

On the other hand, there are Christian groups who go too far the other way. They have a distrust and a suspicion of anything reasonable. Religion to them deals with the mysterious only. They make the gospel as crude intellectually as possible. Worship is a kind of emotional orgy. Religion to these people has nothing to do with thought and everything to do with feeling. Blind fanatical belief in an ancient dogma assumes more importance than ethical behavior. And both of these groups have a little truth, and neither of them has learned that the nature of truth is paradoxical. By cutting one part loose from its opposite they make their half-truths false and misleading.

Paul is an example of the way a Christian should combine the foolishness of God with the wisdom of men. His was one of the great minds of all time—the kind that may appear not more than once in several centuries. If any man might trust his mind, Paul could. This was what prevented his accepting the gospel in the beginning. There was too much in Jesus which seemed like nonsense to his mind. Yet the time came when he surrendered to what he frankly confessed was "foolishness." But after the surrender he came to the affirmation that what seemed like foolishness was wiser than his wisdom.

THE PLACE OF WISDOM

Now let us insist, to begin with, that Christianity does not minimize reason. As an illustration, the followers of John Wesley were long accused of a too easy acceptance of ignorance and wild emotionalism. This was because they felt called to serve uneducated people whose emotions sometimes got out of bounds. But John Wesley was an Oxford don and one of the best educated men of his day. He was always at pains to see that things were done decently and in order, so far as that was possible. He used unordained men to preach in the fields and go into the mines, but he prescribed courses of study for them, and he urged every member of his society to read. George Eliot refers to a bricklayer, converted in a Wesleyan meeting, who developed a desire to learn to read the Bible.

In the early days of America the pioneer itinerant preachers carried books in their saddlebags. They were the first traveling libraries. They were often the only contact between the world of culture and the frontier communities. Across this country as churches were built there were small church colleges established, some of which have grown into universities. They were founded by poor and pious people who wanted their children to have the advantages of higher learning. Those who look down upon the Church as being opposed to education have simply forgotten that education came out of the Church.

Not only that, but the standards of the ministry have been raised constantly through the years so that now a college degree is practically a necessity in most churches. Indeed three years of graduate work are generally demanded. Over the years the Christian Church has put more and more emphasis on an educated, well-trained ministry. The exceptions only serve to sharpen the general trend.

There have been many pressures exerted to halt this movement, it is true. When there is a shortage of ministers, some believe that the way to end the shortage is to lower the standards. It is pointed out that the fact a man has a seminary training does not necessarily mean he will be a good minister. That is so! It is also pointed out that the fact a man may lack a seminary training does not mean he will be a poor minister. We agree. But the Church is on the right track when it moves toward higher educational standards for its leadership and resists the pressures urging it in the other direction.

Let every Christian understand there is nothing to be frightened of in education. There are secular, pagan systems of teaching, and we are opposed to them because we believe them false. But we are never opposed to having men think and learn all the facts they can. We believe that God and truth are one. Whenever a man finds truth, he has drawn closer to God, and whenever he has been found by God, he is in the presence of truth. Christianity is realism, and the gospel is in itself an education. It took a plain man like John Bunyan and inspired him to become the author of a masterpiece. The Christian is given a curiosity to learn. He wants to stretch his mind and ability to their capacity.

An older man told me one time that when he was a student, he always attended a certain church. Looking back on the experience, he was of the opinion that it was the most valuable part of his education. There was a working boy who told me that he always listened to a friend of mine because he could learn so much from the sermon. "It is a substitute for a university education," he said.

An old cattleman slipped into a ministerial conference and listened to the preachers complaining that people did not attend church. Finally he could keep silent no longer. Apologizing for speaking in such a learned gathering, he said, "Whenever an old steer won't come up to the feedrack, I always put better feed in the rack." He had a point. The trouble with our pulpits is not too much education in them but too little. The morning worship service should appeal not only to emotions but also to minds. It should be a cultural experience as well as a spiritual experience. There is no conflict between our religion and reason.

The Limitations of Wisdom

But there is a warning which needs to be given. The gospel is very much aware of the temptations that come to the educated man, and it is conscious of the limitations of reason. There is a sophomoric attitude that despises everything beyond its power of explaining. There is a materialistic point of view that prefers stubborn denial to getting out beyond its depth. Education, instead of giving us perspective, sometimes makes us unable to see over our own ego.

No one was more aware of these pitfalls into which the wise fall than Kierkegaard. Because we have not escaped the traps of logic, his silent voice speaks to us again. Says he: "Sneaking slowly onward, this common sense eats away the absolute bit by bit, undermining faith in and reverence for it—and then finally perhaps an impatient common sense bursts forth boastfully into speech, loudly proclaiming its wisdom, that the absolute is madness." [1]

One of the temptations of knowledge is complacency. Instead of learning how much we can never know, a man may think he now

[1] *For Self-Examination and Judge for Yourselves*, tr. Walter Lowrie (Princeton University Press, 1944), pp. 168-69.

knows everything important. Instead of realizing that the most he can hope to attain is "a smattering of ignorance," he assumes that anything beyond his comprehension is secondary. The educated man is tempted to attach too much significance to definition. If a thing is defined, he believes it is disposed of. But that is not necessarily true at all. Definitions are very useful things, but they do not solve problems, nor do they necessarily increase a man's power to live adequately. There is a rather general tendency for educational conferences to spend long hours wrangling over precise statements of objectives and then depart with a sense of having really accomplished something. In the meantime no one does anything about achieving the goals so beautifully defined. Woe unto the man who complacently assumes that since he has defined a matter he has dealt with it! We had better learn that definitions are mostly a matter of comparison, and the fundamentals of life are not comparable to anything else. They are unique and hence always beyond the bounds of our definitions.

The educated man who has accepted the assumptions of our materialism is too quick to define the impossible. Miracles are disposed of at once on the basis that there are no such things. Prayer? That is only magical hocus-pocus or a form of autointoxication, says the materialist, because he can find no place for it in his system. How unscientific those enamored with science can be in realms beyond their own narrow fields! The world is full of examples of things accomplished by men too ignorant to know they were impossible. Gillette, of safety razor fame, said that a technical training would have made him unable to believe that such a gadget could ever be perfected. With a gigantic misconception proud men proclaim the limits of possibility, which even God does not allow.

Pride and pretense lie in wait for the conceited. Joseph Parker, famed preacher and builder of the City Temple in London, once remarked he had received a letter informing him that the writer would attend the service the next Sunday to criticize the philosophy of the sermon. He added that he was not so worried when he noticed the man had spelled philosophy with an *f*. This is what may happen to men wise in their own conceits.

This pride makes a man despise common men. Yet the common man is often wiser than his educated brother. He is closer to reality and more aware of ultimate truths. He has not been blinded by too much subtle reasoning. There have been many times when the man in the street was ahead of his leaders in perceiving the moral issues at stake. The American democracy has been held steady through the years by the common man, especially from the rural areas. It is not apparent that the intelligentsia are always right. The education of the mind is certainly important, but a heart that is sensitive to moral values and the demands of character is fundamental. It is a good man rather than a brilliant man who is the foundation of any society.

Well-trained men often fall into the pit of despising the man who lacks formal training. The preacher who has had the advantage of seminary will do well to sit at the feet of the man whose training came from his love for people and his desire to serve them. The doctor should be careful not to raise a barrier against the healing ability of the unorthodox. The social worker must beware of a tendency to make procedure more important than results. Rules are useful, but there are times when they must be broken in order to serve a higher law. The little, proud, trained man may prefer not to do anything at all if it cannot be done according to his blueprints. The gospel is very much aware of all these temptations of the educated, and it is suspicious of intellectual pride.

All of this was satirized by Professor A. S. Eddington of Cambridge. He wrote:

I am standing on the threshold about to enter a room. It is a complicated business. In the first place I must shove against an atmosphere pressing with a force of fourteen pounds on every square inch of my body. I must make sure of landing on a plank travelling at twenty miles a second round the sun. . . . I must do this whilst hanging from a round planet head outward into space, and with a wind of aether blowing at no one knows how many miles a second through every interstice of my body. The plank has no solidity of substance. To step on it is like stepping on a swarm of flies. Shall I not slip through? . . .

Verily, it is easier for a camel to pass through the eye of a needle than for a scientific man to pass through a door. And whether the door be barn door or church door it might be wiser that he should consent to be an ordinary man and walk in rather than wait till all the difficulties involved in a really scientific ingress are resolved.[2]

Jesus said that God hides some things from the wise and understanding.

The Foolishness of the Gospel

Another thing to say is that the gospel often seems to be foolishness, and the wiser we are, the more this is true. Most of us have lost this sense of the foolishness of the gospel, and we have no longer a feeling of being intellectually outraged by its demands. But that is because we have allowed our familiarity with it to deaden our sense of its dramatic, upsetting nature. We read the New Testament, and we accept the most startling statements with about as much excitement as we listen to a weather report. The words rake over our minds with the teeth upward. We have listened too often and too dully.

The parts that would still be disturbing to us we water down. Through long practice we have learned how to soften the hard sayings and intellectualize the wild foolishness. To the commands which go contrary to our worldly wisdom we add footnotes and thus force them into the mold we want them to fit. We find it easy to believe that Jesus never meant anything unreasonable. Therefore, where his words have that suggestion, we assume that he was using Oriental imagery. One of the things which we demand that the institution of the Church should do for us is to limit the iconoclastic tendencies of the gospel.

Yet when we look back to the New Testament with fresh vision, we cannot escape the conclusion that its teaching seemed like

[2] *The Nature of the Physical World* (New York: The Macmillan Co., 1928), p. 342.

foolishness, not to say madness, to many people who heard it first. When Jesus returned to Nazareth and preached in the synagogue, he was regarded as one who had become unbalanced. That he should dare declare, "Today hath this scripture been fulfilled in your ears" (Luke 4:21), filled the congregation first with amazement and then with wrath. They were sure this young man, whose family they all knew, must be suffering from delusions of grandeur. They would have killed him had he not gone from them.

Paul confesses in the first chapter of First Corinthians that the gospel was a madness to a great number of people who heard him preach. To the Jews, he says, the gospel was a stumbling block. It is not difficult to understand why. They were the inheritors of a long tradition and a great dream. There would come one day a Messiah. But a crucified criminal the Messiah? Of course not! How could they be expected to understand this strange, insane idea? How well Paul knew that to preach Jesus as the Messiah was to place a stumbling block before the Jews! That was putting it mildly.

But it was no better when he preached to the Greeks. They were the inheritors of the great philosophical tradition. How could the children of Socrates and Plato be expected to believe that a man on a cross could bring God's salvation to them? That God should in some strange way bring redemption through the suffering and death of Jesus was too ridiculous to merit any serious consideration. The Greeks were masters of the art of thinking. They knew all the subtle trickeries of dialectic. But this was so contrary to all of their wisdom that Paul confesses it was "unto Gentiles foolishness."

Then as if this were not enough, the Romans found the gospel hard to accept. In the book of Acts there is the story of the Roman official Festus. With eloquence Paul made his defense and explained his faith, but Festus' reaction was, "Paul, thou art mad; thy much learning is turning thee mad." (Acts 26:24.) Everywhere he turned Paul was faced with the opposition and the hatred of the wise. Each group had something within its philosophy to make difficult the acceptance of Jesus. Christianity demanded that for the sake of Christ men must become as fools in their own eyes.

We have not changed very much in nineteen centuries. We speak glibly about being a Christian nation, and our politicians quote the Bible. But when it comes to taking the gospel seriously, we are as reluctant as the first century. Ask the militarists to accept an American foreign policy based on establishing confidence and good will, and see what they answer. The time has come when we are so dominated by the idea of force that even to suggest a possibility for peace and reconciliation is to be branded un-American. Suggest that we must capture the heart and the imagination of the common man throughout the world instead of bribing him, and see how quickly you are accused of impractical idealism. Will Christianity work as the basis of a foreign policy? Apparently we do not believe it for a moment.

Or turn to our domestic policies. What about the many obvious denials of civil rights? The very fact that the whole matter has become a political issue shows how little we have been willing to take Jesus seriously. Brotherhood? A fine phrase for patriotic addresses, but please do not expect us to practice it. Racial equality? Of course, except where there is a custom and a profit in treating members of some minority as second-class citizens. It must be one of the most tragic of God's experiences to see that after almost two thousand years his Son is still a stumbling block and foolishness to Christian men.

The gospel is a disappointment to worldly minds. Even the mind that is tinged with idealism finds the teachings of Jesus contrary to prudent considerations. A man may desire to be a good employer or a good political representative. But he cannot believe that the Sermon on the Mount describes the necessary qualifications of such a man for such a time as this. Or a man may desire spiritual sensitivity. But he can hardly escape thinking of such a state in aristocratic terms. Surely, he thinks, it is not for the man in the street, and it cannot be obtained by common men. It must be sought by withdrawing from practical affairs and finding the leisure for contemplation. The New Testament's insistence that the spiritual experience is the reward of service seems mad. Even the good men of the world find a radical element in the gospel. Until they have overcome this prejudice against the foolishness of Jesus' way, they keep the barriers up and they keep themselves outside, too wise to be "taken in." When we meet a man who, with simplicity of mind, has accepted the gospel's "foolishness," we admire him and are moved by him, but we are also embarrassed by him.

A Higher Wisdom

Finally, the gospel reveals itself as a profound wisdom too deep for our little logic. That which seemed to be utter nonsense turns out to be divine sense. Much mystery and perplexity remain and must always remain, for we are men, not gods. But at last, finding ourselves laid hold of by God's love given through Christ, we commit ourselves to his "foolishness." Always there is the necessity for loyalty to something beyond our complete comprehension. That is what we mean by faith. It goes on from where reason ends, and through mystery it leads to life.

It is this element in Christianity that makes it contrary to so much of our worldly wisdom. It is seen best in the parable of the last judgment. The goats cannot understand the decision. "What do you mean, Lord, putting us over here?" they ask. "You are mixed up. We are the good people. Don't you remember? We preached some fine sermons. We belonged to the important civic committees. We were on the board of directors of the Chamber of Commerce and the service clubs. We always gave every good cause our verbal support. We were leading citizens."

But the King answers: "I never knew you. Your hearts were hard, and you were ruled by pride. You did not really care for people. You did everything to win the praise of your fellow citizens. You have had your reward."

The sheep, who are also surprised, speak in an embarrassed manner. "Lord," they say, "are you sure you know what you are doing? We lived on the wrong side of the track. Our children were regarded suspiciously by the youth groups organized for nice children. We never had much money."

But the Lord answers, "You cared. You were concerned about men. You thought it was better to help than to succeed." Thus does God reverse things and put the last first and the first last. This is his foolishness over against our wisdom. How many sources of our pride are in his eyes our greatest weaknesses, and how many things for which we are ashamed are in his mind the eternal things!

There is an old story about an Irish missionary who went to Switzerland. One day as he preached to the people, he told them that martyrs were the best intercessors for men at the throne of God. They were a literal people, so they killed him that he might be their intercessor. But the wonderful thing about the story is that it worked. They became Christians. So it is that God attains his victories out of our defeats. With his simplicity he overrides our sophistication. After he has destroyed our confidence in our little wisdom, he redeems us with his foolishness, which is wiser than men.

V

JUDGMENT AND FORGIVENESS

And cast ye out the unprofitable servant into the outer darkness.
—Matt. 25:30
And Jesus said, Father, forgive them; for they know not what they do.
—Luke 23:34

THERE WERE TIMES WHEN JESUS SEEMED TO BE COMPLETELY unyielding in his attitude toward the transgressor. Often they were in connection with failures which we would find it fairly easy to condone. That a man should be severely judged for merely playing it safe and staying neutral is hard for us to understand. Was not Jesus unnecessarily severe with the servant who buried his talent instead of using it? Were not his words too bitter when he described the Pharisees?

Yet there are other times when we cannot understand his willingness to show mercy. On the occasions when it would seem beyond our ability to forgive, Jesus shows a kindness that seems unlimited and beyond human comprehension. Perhaps the crowning example is his word from the cross, "Father, forgive them; for they know not what they do." How could a man in the painful agony of death forgive the fickle crowd which one day had hailed him as Messiah and then turned on him like a beast? It is because Jesus knew how to keep the balance between judgment and forgiveness. We need to be taught by his spirit how to believe in judgment and at the same time practice forgiveness.

The establishing of this balance is one of the most difficult things we are called upon to do. We have seen what happens if the two things are separated. Forgiveness without judgment becomes sentimental and weakening. It destroys the moral life and wrecks the human spirit. It is softness and degradation. But judgment without forgiveness also destroys moral values. A strict justice can become the most unjust thing in the world. As long as we are men, we must believe that our legal systems will destroy us if they are not tempered with mercy.

A judge who takes his position seriously learns the truth of this paradox. There are times when he can be just only by being lenient. There are times when punishment, according to the letter of the law, makes the law a mockery. But the judge has a duty to perform, and he has sworn to uphold the laws of the community. A laxness on his part can also make a mockery of the law. How does he find a working balance?

Parents learn of this problem very early. Children who know that no penalty is attached to wrongdoing become unmanageable and unlikeable. Worse than that, the time comes when they must learn that life and society will not make the allowances their parents made. Too often the result is irreparable tragedy. Yet children need love. If they cannot have confidence in the understanding forgiveness of their parents, they are forever marked. Many a teacher finds that he makes his greatest contribution by restoring some kind of working relationship between the ideas of justice and mercy. There are too many children who never learn this in their homes.

INEVITABLE JUDGMENT

Christianity regards history as a revelation of the working of moral principles. The Hebrews were urged by their religious leaders to consider their own past and the past of their neighbors. They were never allowed to forget that history is the record of God's judgments. There were no exceptions to that, and in the minds of Israel's teachers, being the Chosen People never meant being excused from God's justice. There was no way to escape this inevitable process. Bigness was no protection, nor was success. History reveals, according to the Old Testament, that God is not a respecter of persons or nations.

The prophets kept this before the people. They were in continual conflict with the rulers and politicians over this matter. The political leaders wanted to depend on alliances and military might. The prophets were against all such arrangements when they went contrary to righteousness, as they usually did. In their minds the temporary advantage of power was never to be chosen over doing what was right. For the evil act must one day be paid for by Israel as well as by Babylon.

Christians inherited this faith. Jesus never seeks to encourage his followers with the promise of a way around this inevitable judgment. He weeps over the city because it has chosen death instead of life. "Therefore be ye also ready; for in an hour that ye think not the Son of man cometh," he warns. (Matt. 24:44.) He says to the weeping women whose sympathy went out to him as he was on his way to be crucified, "Daughters of Jerusalem, weep not for me, but weep for yourselves, and for your children." (Luke 23:28.) This deed, he is saying, will bring punishment. If a man would find a denial of the inevitability of judgment without exception, let him not seek it in the teaching of Jesus. Paul was speaking the mind of Christ when he gave this principle its classic statement, "Be not deceived; God is not mocked: for whatsoever a man soweth, that shall he also reap." (Gal. 6:7.)

Now it is too easy to forget this eternal truth. We make our political decisions as if we were facing a fresh situation. But each situation is full of judgments which are coming upon us now for our previous deeds. Every international crisis is full of chickens coming home to roost. It is sheer idiocy to assume that all of our past injustices no longer count and that they do not affect the contemporary attitudes. The unreasonableness of a people is often due to its memory of past treatment. Until we are aware that all of us have contributed to the present situation, we cannot begin to deal with it realistically. Atonement has to be made for the injustices of yesterday, and no people can escape the responsibility for that atonement.

This is all quite clear in the material realm to a scientific generation. Science is to a large extent a discipline which traces the relationship between cause and effect. When it sees the same cause followed by the same effect enough times, science assumes a law of nature which is a generality based on many observations and accepted on faith. No scientist ever assumes that the law will vary for the convenience of a Republican or a Methodist. Under the same conditions it works the same for every man.

Let no man forget this as it applies to him personally. We cannot begin today as a new-born soul. We begin today with the judgments of yesterday crowding in upon us and demanding payment. We are too much like alcoholics who take more drinks than are good for them and say they will not count this one. Life will not be so treated; every one is counted. Yet in the spiritual realm we have the greatest difficulty in accepting the truth of that same principle. There is always the hope that we are exceptions or that we can find some way to circumvent the law. Then when we fail, we feel ourselves badly used. But the Christian with his eyes opened to the implications of his faith will never be thus blinded. As a literary critic said, he will begin every day with the feeling that he is on trial for his life and will probably not be acquitted.[1] For the Christian knows that he stands always under the judgment of a God who makes no exceptions.

A MORAL UNIVERSE

This means, of course, that we live in a moral universe. All of life has to be brought into the harmony of this discipline. Our freedom is limited by the moral demands of life, which is to say the moral law often seems to be an obstacle standing in the way of our attaining what we want. No generation has ever been faced with this more acutely than ours. How we wish that security could be attained on some other basis than justice! If it were only a matter of power or money, we could deal with the problem easily. America with her armed force would find no difficulty in solving

[1] Van Wyck Brooks, *Opinions of Oliver Allston* (New York: E. P. Dutton & Co., 1941), p. 30.

any problem on a power basis. America with her wealth would not be troubled by any problem that demands cash. But the pressing dangers of the time do not seem amenable to these solutions. We know in our clear moments that there is no security until we as well as our rivals are willing to make the radical changes which justice demands.

To the individual there comes the same sense of frustration when he faces the implications of a moral order. How often we think we see a quick way to attain our desires if we did not have to reap what we sow. There are opportunities for thievery and deceit which come to every man. For the moment he may be blinded with the profit to be obtained quickly. But if he is realistic about the matter, he will know that he must not be duped by this temptation. For when we look with clear eyes, the slower way of rightness is the best way. But the man who does not feel from time to time that the moral law is a barrier to his quick success is very rare indeed.

If we think we can ignore this obstacle in our day, it is because we are under the control of the "terrible simplifiers." For them nothing exists but force. They are like the Communists, who discount all spiritual power. The world seems to such men no more than a battleground for physical struggles. It is a terrible moment for a people when they lose their ability to see that policies must rest, not upon force, but upon ethics. For then they will blunder to their doom.

But if the moral order is an obstacle, it is also a great assurance. Like the sea it can swallow ships, but it can be also a highway to the haven of our hopes. For while it can be terrible in its destructiveness, it is mighty in its power to uphold and protect. It sows within evil the seeds of its own destruction. When goodness trembles before the imposing façade of sin, it is held steady by the knowledge that behind the impressive exterior deterioration is already far advanced. When wrong is on the march and men are sure this time that goodness will be overwhelmed completely, then we take comfort in the certainty that there is no staying power in evil. Righteousness can always weary out wickedness.

This truth keeps us steady when the victory of goodness tarries. Then it is that we give thanks for a moral order which makes no exceptions. Our own resentment fades away before our thanksgiving that here is something dependable upon which we can build. The obstacle has been transformed into a firm foundation. What a great assurance is the moral order!

Woodrow Wilson may have made some political blunders. Yet, as Stimson once put it, his mistakes were in the right direction. He saw the essential thing clearly enough, and he had the courage and the devotion to give his life for it. The time came when he saw the League of Nations facing a certain rejection in the United States Senate. But in the midst of his sickness and defeat he could still say, "I would rather fail in a cause I know will one day triumph than to succeed in a cause I know will one day fail." If the moral order is an obstacle to the enjoyment of cheap and easy victories, it is also a vindicator of our noble defeats.

SENTIMENTAL FORGIVENESS

Now if this is true, where does the doctrine of forgiveness come in, and what does it mean? Christians must believe in the certainty of judgment, but they must also believe in the forgiveness of God. Whenever the critic of Christianity gives a superficial glance at these two ideas, he says that only fools can believe in both of them at the same time. Yet this is precisely what we must do.

Because the paradox is never quite hidden from Christians, they sometimes find an answer by saying that God makes exceptions for some men. In their belief they assume that, while the moral order may hold for the sinner, it does not hold for the saint. They believe that for his favorites God breaks the connection between sowing and reaping. This is the cause of much sentimentality in our religion. The austere God who demands holiness, and whose anger is terrible against sin, is transformed into a slightly senile old man who can be manipulated. The sharp outline of one whose ways are not our ways becomes blurred into the image of one who is interesting and weak like us. One of the most blasphemous things we moderns have done is to make the Christian doctrine of the love of God a sticky mess, in which we have drowned his eternal demand for righteousness.

This interpretation of forgiveness transforms Jesus from a stern realist into a sentimental dreamer. It makes him soft and futile. It changes his trumpet call to high endeavor into a lullaby to keep men soothed. It condones the use of the name of Jesus to stir up self-pity. His gospel becomes a siren call to everything that is unworthy in us. It encourages our weakness instead of creating strength. It sends us on a search for ease instead of finding power for the great crusade. It makes the cross of Christ a scapegoat instead of a center of power. The forgiveness that is the abnegation of the moral order is one of the most dangerous heresies that has ever attacked the faith.

The result of this false doctrine is one of the most unlovely by-products of Christianity, namely, the whining Christian. He is the man who thinks that his religion has given him a special claim on life. Nothing bad should ever happen to him now, and if it does, he will whine about how he did not deserve it. The Church exists only to serve him. His minister and fellow church members ought to drop everything at any time to get him out of the difficulties his own selfishness has created. He is so self-consciously good that he assumes God ought to make exceptions for him.

In time of war there are repeated the old stories of special protection for Christians. There is the man who carried a New Testament over his heart, and it deflected a bullet and saved his life. Let us dispose of this nonsense by saying that a deck of cards would have done the same thing. If this good man's life was saved by the prayers of his pious brethren at home, then how do you explain the death of better men? The idea of a special protection which operates according to the goodness of the individual raises more questions than it answers. All of this is magic instead of religion, and certainly it is a perversion of the Christian faith.

When men accept the belief that exceptions will be made for them, they often think they are excused from ordinary ethical

63

behavior. The meanest man I ever knew was also the most out-wardly pious man in the town. His testimonies at prayer meeting rolled out with assurance. His prayers were monotonous, but they were eloquent. Yet he made life unbearable for his family, and his business dealings were a scandal. Was it to such as these that Jesus referred in the parable of the last judgment? Was he classing with the goats all those who assumed they had special claims on him? Could it be that the surprised men invited over on the right side with the sheep were the quiet folk who expected no special favors? Were they the ones whose families loved them?

One of the besetting sins of writers is an unwise tenderness bestowed on the hero or the heroine. These paragons of virtue are allowed to slobber their way through a story until the reader wants to scream. The minor characters are allowed to suffer realistically, but the author's darlings are wrapped in cellophane lest they be touched by the harsh reality of life. Such writers cannot even stop there. They must fill a book with purple passages, as if their softness cannot be confined to characters alone but must affect words and paragraphs.

It is not so with God. His love is too real and too high. The saints who bear testimony to his goodness and concern are like Allen Gardiner of Patagonia. After a lifetime of suffering and persecution he closed his diary with these words, "I am over-whelmed with a sense of the goodness of God." We do not learn forgiveness from a man who was insulated from suffering, but from a man on a cross. There is nowhere the slightest indication that Jesus expected for himself or promised to his followers the negation of the moral law.

Christian Forgiveness

If forgiveness is not making exceptions for Christians, what is it? How does it operate? What difference does it make? The expe-rience of forgiveness in Christ is the assurance that God cares what happens to us. It is the certainty that we can never drift beyond his concern. Alexandre Vinet, in commenting on the Epistle to the Romans, said, "Faith does not consist in the belief that we are saved; it consists in the belief that we are loved." It is amazing what a man can endure if he knows that somebody cares. It is astounding how suffering redeems when the sufferer knows that someone enters into that suffering with him. To reap what we have sown is always redeeming when we have been forgiven. It is this experience which strengthens us, cleanses us, and purifies us. Forgiveness gives the whole process a meaning.

God's forgiveness is the lifting of an intolerable burden. It is guilt that makes progress impossible. The man with unforgiven sin in his heart never dares to be honest. Because he is under the necessity of pretending to be better than he knows he really is, he spends too big a share of his energy covering up the dark places in his heart. He dares not look at himself, and so he dreads to be alone. In the noisy pretense of his living his best possibilities are dissipated. Meant to be on the march, he is always on the defensive. To be forgiven is to be freed from this weight of guilt which so easily besets us. No man can run the race set before him today if he must carry the load of guilt accumulated yesterday. So God in Christ removes that burden as far as the east is from the west.

How much greater is this divine action than saving a man from reaping what he has sown! We are in need of the discipline of the moral order, and if any man could be freed from it, he would be of all men the most miserable. For if there is one thing sure about us, it is that without discipline we disintegrate. Imagine what it would do to any man if he were freed from the demands life makes upon his brethren. Would that result in greatness or saintliness? The answer is obvious. But that a man should bear what others must bear with a greater courage and a sweeter spirit is something full of glory. That a man's suffering should purify his life is a miracle. That a man should learn patience from the experience that drives another man to anger and hatred is a sign of divinity coming into the situation. And this is what happens to the Christian. It is an experience which respects the moral order but transforms the heart.

John Wesley hardly ever preached without describing the lost
state of the human soul. The first part of his sermon was usually
a description of a coming judgment on the sins of mankind. He
relates in his *Journal* an experience of his in Bath:

I preached at Bath. Some of the rich and great were present; to
whom, as to the rest, I declared with all plainness of speech, 1. That,
by nature, they were all children of wrath; 2. That all their natural
tempers were corrupt and abominable; and 3. All their words and
works,—which could never be any better but by faith; and that, 4.
A natural man has no more faith than a Devil, if so much. One of them,
my Lord ————, stayed very patiently till I came to the middle of the
fourth head; then starting up, he said, " 'Tis hot! 'Tis very hot," and got
down stairs as fast as he could.

John Henry Jowett, commenting on this entry, said that Lord
———— should have stayed until Wesley got to the marrow of his
text, "The Son of Man is come to seek and to save that which
was lost." For then he would have learned that over against the
blackness of judgment there is the shining light of forgiveness.
It is one of the great accomplishments of the gospel that it holds
these two seeming opposites together in a divine unity. If we are
strictly judged, we know also the experience of a divine forgiveness.

VI

PERSONAL AND SOCIAL

Save yourselves from this crooked generation.
                                                    —Acts 2:40

For it is he that shall save his people from their sins.
                                                    —Matt. 1:21

ONE OF THE CONSTANT DEBATES WITHIN THE CHRISTIAN CHURCH
goes on between those who believe the gospel is primarily an individual emphasis and those who champion its social implications.
Is my first obligation as a Christian to save myself from a crooked
generation and keep my life untouched by the slow stain of the
world? Or is the primary command of Jesus to serve men? Is Jesus
the Saviour of the individual or of the group? Should Christianity
be concerned with anything beyond helping each man prepare his
soul for heaven? Are wages, hours, housing, compulsory military
training, or liquor control of primary concern to the Church? Must
our faith be relevant to its contemporary social situation?

Of one thing we can be sure, and that is the impossibility of
drawing the line between the personal and the social realms in
human experience. When one watches the sea on a hazy day, it is
sometimes impossible to tell for sure where the sea ends and the
sky begins. So it is with the meeting place of the individual and
the group. To say, therefore, that one can believe in either an individual gospel or a social gospel is sheer foolishness if the gospel is
concerned with all of life. Even more significant is the truth that
each of these aspects of Christianity illumines the other. Until we

can begin to comprehend this interpenetrating unity, we cannot really understand our faith. For so long as we keep apart what must always be held together, we have a distorted view at best. Are these antagonistic viewpoints right? Yes. But they are also wrong, for wrongness is so often not the lie but partial truth.

Each Man Separately

Let us note that the gospel, first of all, comes to each man individually and finds each man's separate soul. In that great moment when a man is found by God in Christ there exists for the time being no other person and no other reality in the world. This is a private experience of the heart. It is personal. We have, to a large extent, lost the sense of this private nature of God's dealing with men. John Galsworthy said there has been a growing tendency in modern novels to lose the sense of the drama of individual character and to substitute the technical analysis of a member of a species. This is done, he thought, without any intention of setting an individual on his legs as a man. It is almost like a professor of biology dissecting a frog for the edification of a class. How different were the older novelists! They had a sense of the utmost importance of each man's life. They looked at the universe through the lives of individuals, and one man's experience became the symbol of something universal. It was in this sense that one man's destiny became significant to each reader.

We have almost lost the sense of the individual nature of pain and anguish. Anyone who has suffered knows that this is one of the most solitary experiences. Around the sufferer there is for a time an impenetrable wall which no other can pierce. Anyone who visits a hospital knows that each sick room is a world of its own. To lose the sense of the terrible and yet splendid isolating nature of pain is to lose the sense of individual personality. But today we have grown accustomed to reading of cities being liquidated or countries starving to death or a nation's children neglected. We are the victims of mass movements and mass thinking. This nearly always happens to irreligious people. For after all has been said, it is the experience of being found individually by God that keeps a man from being overwhelmed by the crowd.

Men are not saved in the mass. Charlemagne's attempt to baptize captured peoples by force and thus spread Christianity more rapidly is the best indication of how little he understood Christianity. Men cannot be converted through the use of force or mass pressure. Men are saved in the secret places of their lives by a power which respects their integrity. Protestantism has held to this truth through all of its life, and this is one of its greatest insights and contributions. We do not believe a man is saved because he belongs to the right church. We do not think the keys of heaven have been given to any individual. We will not agree that any priest can pronounce either doom upon our sins or merit upon our virtues. One of Protestantism's central affirmations is the priesthood of each believer, which is to say that we regard religion as the most individual thing in the world. When a man comes to God, he is not finally dependent on any other human or institutional aid.

Religious education went on the wrong path when it tried to make Christianity an almost automatic process. It was thought that a child might become a Christian and never know he had been anything else. The ideal was to bring young people into the fellowship gently and gradually so that no crisis would occur in their lives. But this approach misunderstood the personal nature of the gospel and the fact that a man has to say Yes to it. He has to know he has been confronted, and he has to know that he has accepted and been accepted. There are two elements which are central in the Christian experience. First, a man hears God say, "Thou art the man." Secondly, he replies, "Thou art my God."

When one reads the testimony of the saints and talks to the great Christians, this certainty of having once been outside and then of having been brought inside is never lacking. They talk about a particular time when they knew that God had put his hand upon them. They differ as to the explanation of the process and the description of the experience, but all of them say as did the blind man who had been healed, "One thing I know, that, whereas I was blind, now I see." (John 9:25.) Nothing about it is automatic, nor can it be. There is a sense in which Christ always finds a man in terms of a crisis.

Something of this is in the background of Goethe's statement concerning his profession as a writer: "I have, in my trade as a writer, never asked myself, How shall I be of service to the world at large? All I have ever done was with the view of making myself better and more full of insight, of increasing the content of my own personality; and then only of giving utterance to what I recognized as the good and the true." And this is true of the Christian. Before he can do anything he has to be something. The first encounter with God is a redeeming experience, private and personal.

Each Man's Worth

Another thing which grows out of this first truth is that the gospel has a deep reverence for the worth and the significance of each man's life. The disjointedness of so much modern living makes us lose sight of this. The radio with its mad mixtures interspersed with vulgar commercials seems to drug some individuals until they forget there is a button which will turn it off. After hours of that mental and moral hash it is no wonder that people have moral and spiritual indigestion. Finally they flee to the movies, which are not true dramas giving us universal insights but brief glittering escapes from reality.

The comic books are a symptom of our disease. At the post exchanges in the last war the combined sales of *Life*, *Reader's Digest*, and the *Saturday Evening Post* were exceeded by the sale of comic books by a ratio of ten to one. The effect of such reading is not to bring meaning to life but to dissipate any slight hints of meaning we may have attained. The digest magazines illustrate the same trend. It may be a good thing to have some magazine articles cut, but the general effect of this reading is to disintegrate our attitudes further. It might be better to take time to read something long enough to obtain a real impression. So many of the reading and entertainment trends of our time result in disjointedness instead of unity. Yet to believe that we are significant we must see our lives in some eternal setting.

No man can read Romans without being profoundly impressed with the depth and breadth of its thought. No other writer wrestles with the mighty problems of human life with more brilliance than does Paul in this great letter. Here is his marvelous insight into the meaning of God, man, destiny, forgiveness, sin, history. The first eleven chapters are mentally exhausting in their concentrated intensity. One feels as if he has witnessed the heroic effort of a great genius to justify the ways of God to men.

Then with all this magnificent sweep of his thought for a background, Paul begins his twelfth chapter with these words: "I beseech you therefore, brethren, by the mercies of God, to present your bodies a living sacrifice, holy, acceptable to God, which is your spiritual service." (Rom. 12:1.) We miss the whole point of the passage if we fail to see that the "therefore" refers to the eleven chapters gone before. Paul is saying in effect, "Because of what God has done and because of what you are, therefore, this is what a man should do with his life." The gospel puts a man's life into its proper setting and rescues it from its disjointedness.

Because each man's life is of eternal significance, we must not expect everyone to be alike. We are wrong when we try to force all men into the same mold. God makes one pattern for each man's life, and then he smashes it. There is no one like you, and there is no person in the world just like any other person in the world. It is too bad that our understanding of this truth is at such a low ebb. For the buffoon tactics of a certain congressional committee would not have been tolerated five minutes by a healthy democracy. Since when is Americanism to be defined as conformity to some reactionary pattern? Americans are bound together by a common love for the principles of this democracy, but within that framework they have the right to be as different as they please. It is about time we informed the embryo demagogues that we do not propose to allow them to smear decent men with the term "un-American" just because they happen to disagree with them.

71

Nor should we expect all the nations we call friendly to have the same kind of democracy we have developed. It would be a sad day if America decided to hold back all aid from any nation which refused to model its government after ours. Democracy in Britain will be different, as it should be. France will have a democracy differing from Italy's. One world does not mean one political system. A people dedicated to the idea of uniformity is a people in the image of the Nazis. It can never claim the American heritage.

Did we fight the war to make everybody like us? Did our young men die so that we or any nation might tell other nations the kind of society they must organize? If my memory is accurate at all, we fought the war to prevent that very thing from happening. We wanted to maintain the basis of free choice. We fought to keep any nation from being in a position to force its pattern on all the rest of the world.

When the Constitutional Convention met in Philadelphia in 1787, all visitors were kept out, and deliberations were in secret. As was to be expected, rumors began to circulate after a time. On August 18 the convention found it advisable to release the following statement in the *Pennsylvania Herald*:

We are well informed that many letters have been written to the members of the federal convention from different quarters, respecting the reports idly circulating, that it is intended to establish a monarchical government, to send for the Bishop of Osnaburgh, etc. etc.—to which it has been uniformly answered, "tho' we cannot, affirmatively, tell you what we are doing; we can, negatively, tell you what we are not doing—we never once thought of a king."

They were not thinking of a kind of government where anyone would have the right to define for others what they must do and think. There is no clearer sign that the founding fathers were aware of the Christian foundations and desired to build on them. Men are never to be regarded as creatures of the state. It is the other way around—the man is first and the state is his servant. Each man has a right to have his individuality respected.

No Solitary Christianity

But the next thing that needs to be emphasized is that no man can be a Christian alone. This is where we move inevitably from the personal into the social. This is one of the difficulties in being a Christian. If only a man could be a Christian by himself, it would not be so hard. If only we might have a wall thrown about us to protect us from the world after our souls have been redeemed. But that is never possible for the disciples of Jesus.

Persons are created and maintained by their relationships, which is to say that society is necessary for personality. Observers of conditions in the Balkans point out that the re-education of children after the war was one of the most difficult tasks facing those countries. Some of the youngsters had been living like wild animals in the woods. Many had seen sights too horrible for human beings to see. Many of them had killed. To make them persons again society must bring them back into decent relationships. Men must not be left to themselves, and we should not forget that you are dependent upon me, and I am dependent upon you for the maintenance of our human status.

The fundamental realities of our lives are human relationships, because the universe rests upon a personal order. Whenever we have personal relations, we are in the presence of absolutes. It is the insight of the gospel that nothing goes right for us until this truth is established and accepted. Jesus talks about our Father in heaven, and he teaches us to regard every other inhabitant on this globe as a brother, a sister, a neighbor. Because as a Christian I am aware of my own worth. I am bound to deal with my brethren, not as if they were means, but as if they were ends. For that is what they are.

This necessity of relationship accounts for the birth of the Christian Church. Let us be clear about one thing—Jesus did not organize the Church. Roman Catholicism's insistence that there is a divine organizational form and that Christ chose one man as the head of all the faithful is nonsense. The scriptural foundation used to justify the pope is the shakiest thing imaginable, and apparent only to men with preconceived ideas. Early Christian groups organized in different ways according to their local situations. Nothing in the New Testament indicates that minute directions for church administration were ever given. Henry P. Van Dusen summed it up admirably in these words:

A first prerequisite is the abandonment, once and for all, of the widely held myth of an original "undivided Church." History recognizes no such reality. Our earliest accounts portray a considerable number of individual, autonomous, and contrasted Christian *koinonias*, or communities (congregations), differing markedly in organization, polity, worship, and even doctrine.[1]

Jesus did not organize the Church, but he did something vastly more—he created it. Out of his teaching there came the longing for fellowship. Men who had sat at his feet knew that a redeeming fellowship was the hope of the world and the only way a society could be saved. The unity of the fellowship was to be in the spirit and not in the form. As a matter of fact, Jesus attacked the religious institution of his day because it had become a vested interest instead of a spiritual power.

We cannot escape the Christian judgment which tests men's personal lives by their social relationships. This is a truism to anyone who takes the time to study the New Testament, but it is one of the most neglected doctrines of our faith. We continue to honor men who are individually moral but socially pagan. We are called upon to be good men, but our goodness is hollow unless it works for a better life for others.

The test of the Church is the kind of society it creates or tolerates. The life of my city is a constant judgment on the life of my church. To the extent that our civic life is corrupted the Church is a failure. To the extent that war is accepted as a way to solve international disputes the Church is inadequate. It is still true that men and their institutions are to be judged by their fruits. Albert Schweitzer said that our civilization is doomed because the

[1] World *Christianity* (New York and Nashville: Abingdon-Cokesbury Press, 1947), p. 69.

Church has lost its power. How did he know? Because there was a First World War, and religion, he said, having lost its purity, had now lost its authority.

There has come down to us a poem over a hundred years old, written by Runeberg, one of Finland's greatest poets of the nineteenth century. He tells the story of a peasant and his wife who were trying to win a living from a mountain homestead. The harvest was destroyed the first year by floods, hail, and frost. To keep alive they mixed bark with the little meal they had salvaged. After a promising season the second year everything went wrong again, and the harvest was lost. They had to double the portion of the bark in the meal. But the third season was entirely successful, and the harvest was excellent. In her joy the wife said, "Now we can throw away the bark meal and use the rye flour only." But her husband took her hand and said gravely, "We must still mix the bark with our flour, for the frost has destroyed our neighbor's grainfield." And there you have it! Am I a Christian because I am by myself fairly decent? Is it enough not to do evil to others? No, the reality of my Christian character is measured by my concern for my neighbors.

A CHRISTIAN SOCIETY

The final thing to see is that we are called upon to build the kind of society which recognizes each individual man's worth. We are not to be mere defenders of the way things are. The fearful respect which so many Christians have for the ethics of the established order is a scandal. Christians were never supposed to assume that public opinion is the court of last appeal. We are supposed to be in the vanguard of those who have caught a vision of a better society, which is to say a society that has established justice as its ruling passion.

It should be said that this kind of social life will not make everybody happy. Some will have to give up things which they would like to keep. But no man shall have the right to prosper at the expense of his fellow. Some will find their private domain invaded, and matters which they would like to settle without consultation

75

will be decided on a broader basis. Whenever each man's dignity is assumed, his own behavior will have to be modified. Nobody can have all that he would like to have. It is no wonder that the social gospel seldom receives the cheers of the comfortably satisfied.

But the test which Christianity applies to every way of life is the extent to which it regards each man as an end in himself. This is the central thing about a social organization rather than a label. Christians are never too concerned with what a thing may be called if it measures up to this test. Capitalism, free enterprise, the American way are all under the judgment of the Christian criterion. It ought to be recognized that shouting "socialist" or "communist" at any attempt to broaden the base of human rights is a shabby trick that should fool no thinking man. Let us not be so naïve as to assume that the right label is to be preferred over reality. Too often a label is used like a scarecrow to frighten away the fearful and the stupid.

In recent days there has grown up a literature of Communist disillusionment. A great number of people gaily assumed that here was the answer. But when they observed a needless cruelty which they had never seen before, they gradually lost their enthusiasm. People who have had a Christian environment cannot endure the ruthlessness which has characterized Communism's treatment of individual dignity. No people once touched with Christianity's sense of individual worth can accept a social system which denies it. For whether they like it or not, they have learned to accept that Christian standard.

The social implications of the Christian experience break forth constantly. Thus a man like Paul can never long keep away from this most practical side of the Christian teaching. After wrestling with the most profound of theological issues, before he has finished, he will break in with something like this: "Now we that are strong ought to bear the infirmities of the weak, and not to please ourselves. Let each one of us please his neighbor for that which is good, unto edifying." (Rom. 15:1-2.) That is what we cannot escape.

God has spoken to each man's separate soul, it is true. But when that happens, somehow we are more sensitive to the call of our brethren. We hear them say, "We think you will come. We are expecting you. We need you." So this whole experience cuts across all our futile attempts to distinguish between the individual gospel and the social gospel. There is only the gospel. There is only one great experience and one great commission for Christians. "As thou didst send me into the world even so sent I them into the world," said our Lord. (John 17:18.)

VII

SORROW AND JOY

In the world ye have tribulation: but be of good cheer.
                                        —John 16:33

WHEN ONE READS LUKE'S STORY OF THE NATIVITY, HE IS AWARE OF tremendous contrasts which have been drawn. There is the darkness of the little town contrasted with the light of the heavenly hosts and the star. There is the crowded inn where there was no room for the humble folks from Nazareth and the open sky with its angel visitors. There is the shuddering fear of the poor shepherds and their intense joy as they hear the angels' message which is to drive out all fear. Here at the very birth of Jesus Christ the artist has drawn these contrasts between sorrow and joy which men must know. The life of Jesus illustrates this constant variation. He is indeed the man of sorrows and acquainted with grief. Yet, as one reads his teaching, there is his brilliant satire, which must have brought a smile to the lips of all those who heard him. There is his desire to be with people and to be in the midst of children. The verse in John which reads, "Jesus wept," is not put there because it is characteristic, but because it is news. It represents an exception. There is in his whole life an amazing blend of the sorrow of the world and an unspeakable joy.

Men always try to flee from sorrow in order that they may find a constant pleasure. Men like Swinburne, for example, bewail the fact that upon the world the breath of the "pale Galilean" has fallen. Yet, strangely enough, when they create a life without him, their paganism turns into the dark night of despair which is un-lighted by any hope. In some strange way the gospel with its sorrow makes it possible for men to know the heavenly joy which it offers. But you cannot have one without the other. The failure of paganism is its inability to understand this. A philosophy which assumes the possibility of endless pleasure is doomed to defeat. As there can be no light without shadow, so there can be no joy without grief. To find a way of life which will prevent our sorrow from destroying our faith and keep our humor from turning sour is a fundamental human need.

Pagan Sorrow

We should begin by considering the useless pagan sorrow which is characteristic of so many people. It is an entirely negative thing, for any sadness that is not accompanied by repentance or does not urge us toward a concrete restitution is simply bad. It prevents a better kind of life, and it prevents any constructive purpose from having its way. It casts over all human effort a kind of pall, and the future becomes dismal and unchallenging because it is looked at through this gray fog. A pagan sorrow is like the crying of a child who wants something that he really ought not to have. It is like a child's tantrum, which means no more than that his will has been thwarted for the time being. There is no dignity in it, because there is no facing of reality. It will not make a man better, but it can make him much worse. It is a sorrow that comes when men refuse to face the inevitable. They cry against the luck or the chance which seems to deny them what they would like to have just now. It shows a lack of perspective and a failure to comprehend what the human situation really is. It is like a man standing out in the storm and cursing the thunder. It is an immature refusal to adjust life to reality.

Sorrow is sometimes no more than a spoiled resentment against the moral order. It is a whining complaint that life makes no exceptions. It is anger expressed against reaping what a man has sown. Too much of the sorrow of men falls into this category and represents this essentially childish thing. It does not strengthen; it weakens. Instead of opening a man's eyes to reality pagan sorrow prevents his seeing life whole. He loses sight of all of the good in human life, and the whole world seems to be evil. His perspective is gone. His spirit, instead of becoming more aware of the suffering of others, is dulled to all others and their needs.

Here are some lines by Harry Kemp which express this pagan blindness:

> The Spring blew trumpets of color;
> Her Green sang in my brain—
> I heard a blind man groping
> "Tap—tap" with his cane;
>
> I pitied him his blindness;
> But can I boast, "I see"?
> Perhaps there walks a spirit
> Close by, who pities me,—
>
> A spirit who hears me tapping
> The five-sensed cane of mind
> Amid such unguessed glories—
> That I am worse than blind.[1]

This is the experience that comes to the man who indulges in a useless sorrow. It is a blighting experience, and it is this kind of sorrow which is unendurable, because it destroys faith.

CHRISTIAN SORROW

The people who care very little about us are always willing for us to have what we want rather than be hurt. It is always the man or the woman who loves us most profoundly who is willing to see us suffer rather than betray our best selves. It is with our own children that we are exacting and demanding. Acquaintances like us but let us alone. Our wives love us and will not let us alone. The

[1] By permission of the author.

nagging husband or wife is sometimes one who is unable to harmonize the way the other person is with an exalted image that he has created not wisely but too well. God is love, says our religion, and that means that he is something much more than easygoing kindness. Because he does not look upon us with contempt, we know that his sorrow for us in our failure is the most tragic thing in the world. We also know that somehow the sorrow of God redeems us. This is the saving sadness of Christianity.

Christian sorrow ennobles men, for it has within it the Godlike desire for men to be their best. As a matter of fact, the root of Christian sorrow lies in our failure, and the failure of all mankind. We are disappointed men once we have caught the vision of what we ought to be as God's sons, and we always know a kind of sadness in our hearts.

The difference between these two kinds of sorrow is illustrated by the deaths of Adolf Hitler and Abraham Lincoln. One could never think of Hitler as anything but a man defeated because he wanted what he had no right to have. Hitler in defeat was not a noble figure, for in that defeat he revealed, for all the world to see, the evil and cheapness of his philosophy. When one looks at Abraham Lincoln, however, one sees the saving sorrow of sacrifice. One can read it in his face. Lincoln was sorrowful, not because he could not have his own way, but because he was caught in a situation filled with all the tragedy of a broken society. Something about Lincoln's sorrow was redeeming, not only to the man himself, but to his people. If he had gone down in defeat, still there would have been in him a nobility which would have been healing, both to his enemies and to his friends. His death was redemptive, and the nation's mourning for him was one of its greatest moments.

Christian sorrow always brings a new appreciation of humanity. It does not make us despise our brethren. It makes us want to share their sorrow. For when there comes to the Christian a defeat in life, it creates an understanding of how many men have had the same experience, and even worse ones. When a man is sad as a Christian ought to be sad, he enters into a new and more vital relationship with all mankind. Christian sorrow broadens the vision of men, for it builds within them a new sympathy. This is what Jesus meant in the Beatitude, "Blessed are they that mourn: for they shall be comforted." He is not merely putting a premium on mourning. He is saying that the man who can mourn and who is able to know sorrow is to be thought of as a blessed man, because he shall find comfort in his sympathy for his brethren. He is saying that sharing is more satisfying than merely defending, and it is this exhilaration which only the humble know.

How true it is that the man who has suffered is the first to come to the assistance of the wronged! It is the untouched who do not know how to help the wounded. Unlike pagan sorrow, which oftentimes makes a man withdraw from others, Christian suffering makes him quick to hear the cry of need. I am not sure that this exegesis is legitimate, but it has always seemed to me that the good Samaritan himself must have at one time fallen among the thieves. He had been where that wounded man was, and he was quick to feel his pain. Because he knew what it meant for a man to be in that situation, the Samaritan responded immediately.

An African native one time used a most illuminating phrase in speaking of the Cross. Said he, "The Cross of Christ condemns us to be saints!" He was saying that somehow out of the suffering of Christ and the suffering of Christians there is not only a demand that we become better but also the aid to become better. It is the Cross which is the indispensable element in man's being redeemed through suffering. Without it his pain has no significance, and he feels only a dull resentment that things had to be that way. But in the Cross of Christ the man who walks through the valley of the shadow finds himself ennobled.

Pagan Joy

If we turn to the other side of the picture for a moment, we need to recognize that there is also a cheap and degrading joy. All of our rejoicing is not worthy of us. Sometimes the man who seems to be happiest is the man who is most to be pitied. There is a kind of rejoicing which is merely a retreat from reality. Men sometimes laugh because they are afraid to face truth. We flee from our best by laughing at it. We degrade our best moments by covering them with a cheap humor. Men sometimes seem to rejoice because they are afraid to mourn. Heywood Broun said that probably, if we knew all the details of the story, Peter denied Christ with a wisecrack. It is oftentimes true that men take the road downward with a laugh and a joke. We would do well to pray constantly, "Lord, save us from a rejoicing which is a betrayal of thee."

The Gospel of John has a great story of a woman at the well of Sychar. You will remember how Jesus came along in the heat of the day and stopped there for a drink. She had the greatest opportunity any individual ever had since time began—a few moments alone with the greatest person the world has ever seen. Yet she spent the time in useless banter and the making of silly, stupid remarks. He asked her for a drink, and she ridiculed him, a Jew, for having to ask a drink from a Samaritan woman. When he told her that he could offer her the water of life, she must have laughed at him as she said, "What are you? A magician? How can you draw water from the well when it is so deep? Are you greater than Jacob who gave us the well?" When he promised her living water, all she could think of was some clever trick which would save her from having to come quite so far after water. When he uncovered the moral need of her life, she tried to escape the uncomfortable turn of the conversation by starting an argument as to whether men ought to worship in Jerusalem or "in this mountain." Only with great effort did he bring her back finally to face the reality of her need and accept what he had to give. She was not the first, nor was she the last, to try to escape the serious implications by a silly smartness and a cheap laughter. The story has a happy ending because Jesus was patient and persistent. It is not always so. Many a man has been successful in warding off a transforming experience by covering himself with a veneer of cheap wit.

This has been true of our time. There is an element of escapism in our laughter and a sadness in our joy. Too often our humor has not helped us to understand, but has helped us to cover up. Historians have noted that before the downfall of cities and societies there has usually been much merriment and apparent joy. But it was not healthy laughter, nor did it recreate. The brittle humor of our time is often cruel. It does not heal; it only stabs. It has been brutal and secular. Instead of showing the vain pretense of the powerful and the proud it has sought to show the stupidity and the clownishness of the weak and the disinherited.

This is to say that much modern humor has no faith in it, and hence has no health in it. There is about it a kind of hectic flush that betrays the patient has a fever and is sick. It has something of the same quality of the drunk who for the moment is having the time of his life, and yet one knows that it is not the real person who is like that. It is merely the alcohol at work temporarily, and when it has worn off, his condition will be worse than ever. We have paid too much honor in our time to the individual with the sharp tongue and the biting wit. We have not understood how this reveals the poverty of our own spiritual situation.

Most of us, in these days of success worship, think of a poor man as one who lacks money. Francis of Assisi, however, thought of a rich man as one who lacked the grace of poverty. So too many of us in our time have thought of the sad individual as one who lacks humor, and sometimes we have failed to comprehend that the so-called humorist betrays, by the type of humor he uses, his own lack of faith and confidence. Paganism reveals itself not only in its useless sorrow but also in its meaningless humor. A secularist movement which is supposed to bring freedom and joy to men only succeeds in bringing to them the bitter laughter of men who have betrayed themselves.

The mad pursuit of personal happiness makes the faithless man consider no higher obligation than his own desires. To him these lines of Richard Lovelace will sound stupid:

> I could not love thee, Dear, so much,
> Lov'd I not Honour more.

Rather, he will applaud the Duke of Windsor when he chooses romance instead of duty. Why should a man not do what he wants to do, even if it does entail abdication and desertion? Yet one wonders if such choices are not regretted, and if a haunting sense of betrayal does not spoil the pleasure. At least it is true beyond debate that when a nation's leaders are willing to sacrifice duty for happiness, it is a sad time for the nation. Pagan joy means public sorrow.

Joy of Christians

But out of the Christian's sorrow there comes what might be called the eternal joy of the saints. A college student once wrote to Harry Emerson Fosdick that he thought being a Christian made life more interesting, but it did not make it more comfortable. The boy was right. The joy of the saints is not a joy that springs primarily out of the experience of comfort. It springs out of the assurance that life has meaning, that it makes sense, and men may have faith in its ultimate significance. Claudel, the French poet, upon hearing for the first time Beethoven's *Fifth Symphony*, said he knew there was joy in the heart of the universe. So those who come to the Man of Sorrows know at last that there is in the universe an ultimate triumph and joy.

There have been some muddleheaded people who thought the Christian gospel frowned upon all material things which brought joy to ordinary men. True it is that in the history of Christianity there have been periods when men have thought they served their Lord best by entering the gray twilight of negation and sadness. Real Christianity, however, is not that and never can be. No other great religion has so much confidence in the possibility of using material things for good. Let us never forget that the doctrine of the Incarnation means that God was willing to reveal himself in a human body. Much of the greatest love poetry in the world has been written by Christians. Never let us be so foolish as to think that when Christianity talks about joy, it talks only about an otherworldly kind of experience entirely divorced from the simple pleasures of this life. Christianity knows that when a man's mind is centered on the ultimate values and his heart is pure, the simple things of his physical life bring him joy.

The joy of the saints is always dangerous to the pretenders. It is the saint who can laugh at the vain show of the worldly. The absurd claims of tyrants and materialists are taken seriously only when a generation loses its religious sense. One of the best examples is Jesus and the Pharisees. The Pharisees, by making the common people take them seriously, could maintain their position and hold a place of honor. They never would have objected too much to Jesus if he had argued with them or debated with them. They could handle that kind of approach, for they had grown very clever in verbal controversy. But when Jesus refused to argue and only satirized and laughed, he became their most dangerous enemy. They could stand almost anything but that. When at last the Pharisees and the priests rose against Jesus, they had decided he was a dangerous man because with his pure heart he could see through all their vain hypocrisies.

Let us learn our lesson from Jesus in this: there are some sins which, if taken too seriously, become more significant then they ought to be. Sometimes our sins can be washed away with laughter. The saint oftentimes escapes some of the besetting sins of other men simply because his perspective makes him understand how ridiculous such things really are. The joy of the saints not only makes their lives happy; it keeps them sane. The Old Testament dares to assert several times that God laughed. The saints are joyful because of their confidence in the ultimate victory of goodness. They know it does not all depend upon them or upon any group of men. They can afford to wait. So we have the strange contradictory situation of the Christian facing what seems to the pagan to be an ultimate defeat and taking it with a quiet confidence. As Disraeli said to the scoffing members of Parliament when his first speech failed, "You will hear me yet."

In that rather strange play of Eugene O'Neill's, *Lazarus Laughed*, men attempt to make Lazarus, who has returned from the dead, tell them about his experience. Across the chasm between them and this man with the unique experience they throw word bridges in the hopes that they too may enter that hidden realm and learn what is there. But it is all in vain. Lazarus cannot answer their questions. He cannot describe his experience. He can only laugh joyously and triumphantly. What is death? His laughter seems to say it is something glorious and splendid. What a wonderful thing it is that to men who know they must die there comes this faith and joy. For laughter is from God and is possible only for men who know the universe has ultimate meanings.

In the days of the Spanish Inquisition every kind of terrible torture that men could devise was used. One of the most subtle forms of suffering contrived was to put a man in a dungeon that was not high enough for him to stand at his full height. He was powerless to stand straight and breathe deeply and hold up his head. This, it was discovered, could break the spirit of a strong man. The world does this to us if we are not careful. Paganism always does it to us, and in spite of all its great promises the time comes when we know we have entered a cell where we cannot stand tall. The Christian faith, beginning with the sorrow of life, leads us finally to the joy of the saints, which helps us to look up and know that beyond the years there is a mighty destiny for each man. The Christian faith brings to human life a redeeming sorrow, which in turn creates a triumphant joy.

VIII

GENTLENESS AND AUSTERITY

Behold then the goodness and severity of God.—Rom. 11:22

THE ABILITY OF WILLIAM BLAKE TO ANALYZE A DIVINE MYSTERY
with a few words is illustrated by the following lines:

> Tyger! tyger! burning bright
> In the forests of the night,
> What immortal hand or eye
> Could frame thy fearful symmetry?
>
> . . . .
> And what shoulder, and what art,
> Could twist the sinews of thy heart?
> And when thy heart began to beat,
> What dread hand? and what dread feet?
>
> . . . .
> When the stars threw down their spears,
> And water'd heaven with their tears,
> Did he smile his work to see?
> Did he who made the Lamb make thee?

Blake observed one of nature's enigmas. We must assume that one
hand made nature, but how shall we explain the same creator as
making the lamb with its gentleness and the tiger with its fierceness? Nature has always these two elements, oftentimes dwelling
side by side. The coming of the spring with its green growing things
and the fresh new color of the flowers makes us feel that nature is

gentle and kind. But there is also a ruthlessness in it and a cruelty. It is often "red in tooth and claw." We cannot begin to comprehend the natural world unless we remember Blake's symbol—the lamb and the tiger.

A balanced society is both lamblike and tigerlike. The people who have transformed themselves into armed camps and made conquest the goal of their existence have all come to a bad end. History does not say that naked force and aggression mean a strong people. Woe unto the nation that has no respect for the gentler arts! Yet it is also true that doom awaits a people who place ease above justice. There are some things we must hate. There are some forces we must oppose with the fierceness of the tiger.

A man's life needs both the tiger and the lamb in it. A man ought to be capable of fierce indignation, and when an easygoing tolerance has dulled his power to hate the right things, he is a sick man. But he needs gentleness too. He needs to be sympathetic and able to enter into the suffering of his brethren. Christianity has this paradoxical effect on men. At one time they are intolerant of sins which the world regards with only mild interest. Yet at other times Christians become reconcilers of the world through the sweetness of their tempers. The important thing for us to note is that the same hand fashioned the tiger which fashioned the lamb, and it is necessary to find a way for them to dwell together without devouring or being devoured.

The criticisms of Christianity reveal these two elements which always dwell within it. There is a considerable body of opinion which regards religion as primarily a warmonger. I can remember yet a huge volume on the shelf of the seminary library labeled The Wars of Religion. In this dark page of church history critics have had wide opportunity for their activities. In fact, when one reads the anti-Christian's report, one gets the idea that if there had been no Christianity in the world, there would have been no wars in the West.

But just as we adjust ourselves to this, we find another school of opponents who attack the gospel because it is too pacifistic. They regard it as a softening influence on the human race, a destroyer of virility. They criticize it for talking too much about turning the other cheek and getting along peacefully with one's adversaries. In confusion the Christian asks himself just what this gospel is—tiger or lamb? It is both. It goes wrong when its champions forget that amazing fact and try to make it only one thing or the other. Christianity is a divine gentleness held in tension by a divine fierceness.

The Gentleness of Jesus

Whenever a war comes along, there is a desperate attempt to make Jesus its spokesman. With sure instinct as to what would help gain the public support for every military venture, Jesus is brought into every propaganda bulletin possible. A verse here or a verse there is wrenched out of its scriptural context and used to give the impression that Jesus would be quite at home with a machine gun and would at the very least participate as a recruitment officer. The attempt of some general to enter the field of Biblical exegesis is one of the amusing things theologians and Bible scholars have to observe. The only thing which saves the matter from a complete blasphemy is the revelation that no man wants openly to confess his way is entirely opposed to Jesus.

But all of this is utterly futile because there lies across such attempts the impenetrable barrier of the Cross. The Cross was not only a stumbling block to the Jew; it is also a stumbling block to the militarist. For if Jesus could ever have been willing to condone force, that time must have been when he was facing execution. Why did he not then call his legions of angels to his aid? Why did he not raise the revolt which was seething under the surface of Palestinian life? Why did he say, "Put up thy sword"? Why did he allow himself to be crucified as a criminal, with his work barely started? If he could believe that the use of force to attain moral ends would ever work, he would have used it then. If we are able to be calm and objective, we know that, because of the Cross, the most ludicrous activity in the world is the attempt to make a militarist out of Jesus.

When we look for men with the spirit of our Lord, we turn to men like Gandhi and Schweitzer. How easy it is to see Jesus leading a people toward freedom by the use of spiritual power! It is not difficult to see him counseling nonresistance. He would be quite at home in an African hospital, ministering to the superstitious natives. We can see him offering himself as a sacrifice for the exploitation suffered by that unfortunate continent at the hands of the white race. But Jesus Christ dropping a bomb? Never!

The Christian centuries have made the teachings of Jesus so familiar that we have grown dull to his amazing tenderness. Yet in the crude and cruel days of the first century how much greater must have been the shock when people listened to the peaceful doctrines of Jesus! What did they think when they heard him say, "Love your enemies, do good to them that hate you, bless them that curse you, pray for them that despitefully use you." (Luke 6:27-28.) What an extreme, almost ridiculous gentleness this must have seemed to those who first heard these words. How upsetting it must have been to men brought up in the strict moralism of the Mosaic law to hear Jesus offer pardon to the woman taken in adultery. For this was not a breaking of the secular law of Rome. It was the breaking of the religious law of the Jews. Was this not the last word in a gentleness that knew no bounds?

We have made much in recent times of the fact that Jesus did not specifically condemn slavery. But in a world where slavery was the foundation of social life his treatment of the disinherited and weak must have seemed radical enough. Children were the property of their fathers. Yet to Jesus it was a child who was to be first in the Kingdom of God. To all the wise and powerful he spoke of the need to become like a little child. Men were not accustomed to the courtesy Jesus showed to the weak. With his deep respect for every living soul he taught that ancient world a lesson in humility that ate like acid into its cruelty.

Albert Schweitzer has become almost a legend in his own lifetime. As a boy he was favored over the poorer boys of the village because of his status as the minister's son. Which is to say he was "a sprig

91

of the gentry." He wrestled one day with one of the village boys and managed to throw him. The boy got up and said that if he could have broth each day like the pastor's son, he would be strong enough to throw him. From then on Schweitzer's soul revolted against his advantages. He would not wear warm clothing while others were cold. He wanted to wear the same rough shoes they wore. He was a problem to his father, who had to punish him for appearing before visitors "unsuitably dressed to his station in life." It was the example of Jesus which made it necessary for him to identify himself with the less fortunate. Far from encouraging men to take what they wanted by force, Jesus' word was, "Give to him that asketh."

CHRISTIANITY AND SOCIETY

The general effect of the gospel on society has been a taming one. Into the realms where jungle law operated it came to alleviate the suffering of the victims. Where cruelty was practiced, Christianity taught God's demand for kindness. Those who have been in non-Christian countries have remarked on the cruel sights which shocked them, such as the mistreatment of animals by the peasants. There seems to come to human beings who have learned a dull acceptance of pain a blind impulse to pass it on to some other creature. The influence of Jesus has been one of curbing this animal tendency. The history of our civilization has been a record of Christianity's infusing its culture with a deeper concern for the exploited. It went to the barbarian hordes who sacked Rome, and laid upon them a restraining hand. The missionary went to the colonies to curb the merchant's lust for gain and give something to native populations, where others went only to take. If it had not been for the missionary enterprise, one wonders what America would mean to Africa and China.

All of this we have taken for granted. But with the coming of the Nazis we awakened to the truth that men are not born with an ideal of kindness. It is something that has to be won against great odds. It is denied by naturalism. Cruelty is glorified by the unredeemed powerful. Hatred is made a virtue by the worshipers of blood and soil. We begin to catch a vision of the heroic proportions of Christianity's conquest. We begin to see that what we now call the marks of the civilized man are, for the most part, the qualities encouraged and developed by the gospel. Our religion came to do something that men were not naturally willing to do. It came to make them share suffering and be more sensitive to it than they had ever been before. No man seeking to escape pain will dare to become a Christian, for the gospel makes each man share his brother's burdens. There is no peace for the Christian so long as one child, one woman, or one man is being wronged. As Ezekiel put it, we must sit where they sit. Many a man has had to revise his attitude of indifference completely after he became a Christian.

A few years ago, as I was preparing a series of lectures on Christianity's influence in Western civilization, a friend of mine offered some very good counsel. "Do not yield to the temptation to ex aggerate," he said. "You will find you do not need to do it. Even with understatements you can make the case for Christianity entirely convincing." He was right. Nearly every merciful institution began in the Church. Where did hospitals, orphanages, free schools come from? Where did the idea arise that no man should starve and no man should be denied medical attention? It all came from the Christian faith. Wherever there was indifference, Jesus taught concern. The difference Christianity has made is the difference between unrestrained cruelty and disciplined service.

One of the best examples of the Christian influence is the story of Telemachus. He was an Asiatic monk, and he went one day to the Colosseum, where the gladitorial fights were to be held. As the gladiators saluted the emperor with the words, "We who are about to die salute you," Telemachus leaped forward and cried, "In the name of Christ, forbear!" They only laughed at him, and the fighters made ready to begin. Then the monk jumped down into the arena and tried to separate the fighters. Good-naturedly they thrust him aside to get on with the entertainment. The crowd enjoyed the spectacle and howled with laughter. But when Telemachus persistently interfered, the crowd became impatient and shouted, "Run

93

him through." There was the flash of a sword, and the monk was dead in the arena, with his blood staining the sand. The games went on, but people began to leave. Somehow the fun had gone out of the show. And it was the beginning of the end. Finally the cruelty of the arena sports was ended, and that black episode was over. Christianity had spoken, and as it grew stronger in influence, Rome's bloody cruelty was ended. The gospel has been a gentle influence on society.

AUSTERITY

Yet we have not really understood Christianity unless we see it also in the light of a severe austerity. Remember Paul's word: "Behold then the goodness and severity of God." (Rom. 11:22.) All those who make our religion merely gentleness have taken one side of the truth and allowed it to get out of hand. The church which announced the installation of rocking chairs was a church in danger of losing its soul. For ours is not a rocking-chair religion.

There is a fierce austerity about the teachings of Jesus which is repellent to the men seeking only relaxation. Consider its ethical standards. The prophetic books of the Old Testament tell the story of a heroic fight to keep Israel sensitive to the holiness of God and loyal to his severe demands. Surrounded by neighbors whose religion was often little more than a series of sexual orgies, the Hebrews were tempted to accept a lax morality. It seemed unreasonable to expect Israel to remain pure when others ignored purity and appeared to get along all right. But the prophets never gave up, though they were often defeated. Jesus was in their tradition when he insisted on a morality that went beyond the strict letter of the law. No one showed a fiercer hatred of sin than did Jesus.

We are often rebellious against the high demands of the gospel. Every great war brings as its inevitable result a lowering of moral standards. People lose their moorings and drift with the tide. In such times Christianity seems hopelessly out of date with its insistence on individual purity and social responsibility. Everyone seems to be doing just the opposite. Christian teaching, which still holds to high and awful standards, appears as something quaint to the sophisticates. Heroes of contemporary literature do not find what they really want, but it never seems to dawn upon the authors that the denial of strict ethical behavior has anything to do with it.

Christianity's demand that one sacrifice personal desires for the good of others seems to many a person too high an ideal. Over against it we place our right to be happy and our right to fulfill our own desires. Very often this means simply doing what we want to do regardless of its effect on others. Of this philosophy Christianity will have no part. It believes there are values more significant than the attainment of selfish goals. No wonder men turn their eyes toward easier ways!

The difference in the viewpoint of the Church and the viewpoint of the world is apparent when we look at marriage. To the sentimentalist romance is the final goal. To the Christian the home takes precedence over individual whims. Brought up on a diet of modern fiction and movies, young people assume that love is one continual thrill, and when it ceases to be that, they consider themselves justified in denying their vows. Back of our broken homes there is the pathetic and immature attempt to hang on to sensations which ought to give way to mature and permanent values. Look at the marriage ritual of the Church and you find such phrases as "in sickness and in health," "for better, for worse," "for richer, for poorer." Why bring these terrible possibilities into the picture? Because they may happen, and if they do, no person is released from his vows thereby. One of my good friends has had an invalid wife for many years, yet I have never heard him murmur or complain. If anyone should ask him why he has continued to carry such a heavy burden, he would reply that he made a bargain which was to be honored "in sickness and in health." The wonderful thing about it is that by accepting the obligation he has created for himself a joy which the selfish thrill chasers can never know. No panaceas will heal our broken homes, but only a return to the realism of this Christian severity.

Goethe wrote: "I can bear much, suffering the most distasteful things sent by the gods with calm courage. But four things I hate like poison and serpents—the smoke of tobacco, lice, garlic, and the Cross." No one likes the Cross. Jesus did not like it. But the Cross is at the center of our faith, for without it we would forget that along with the goodness and gentleness of God's commands is the awful severity of his will.

Gentleness Needs Austerity

Gentleness without austerity becomes soft and characterless. The kind of person who is all sweetness with no steel in him is not inspiring. He has the same effect as eating too many chocolates. Into a minister's office one time came a man so effeminate that the minister confessed he almost asked him his maiden name. There is something unsound in that kind of character. Mercy without strength is not cleansing, and kindness without strength is not admirable.

But on the other hand austerity without gentleness becomes brittle and hard. It is self-defeating. The two things must come together. This demands a miracle of God, for no man knows how to combine these opposites. But the same hand which made the tiger made the lamb, and that same hand can make gentleness and severity dwell together. Each makes the other effective. We remember our mother's hands were the most gentle and healing influence in our life. When we were bumped or bruised, how soothing to feel the touch of her hands. But there may have been other times when we were stretched across her knees, and those same hands wielded a hairbrush. They were anything but soothing then. Her greatness was an influence that was both gentle and austere. So it is with God. So it must be with us.

Christianity separated the sin from the sinner. Toward the sinner it was more forgiving and gentle than any other philosophy had dared to be. But toward the sin it burned with an undying hatred. Toward the sinner it behaved like a lamb, and toward the sin it looked with the ferocity of the tiger. One of the problems of our life is to maintain at high tension and in proper balance these two points of view. Over a period of years we tend to become bitter and cynical toward men. Finally we despise them and look upon them as fit receivers of the lash. But while this is going on, we have grown accustomed to the evil that makes men bad. We no longer want to do anything about it, for we no longer see it clearly. How shall we keep our values straight? Only by having the mind of Christ can we "behold the goodness and severity of God."

It was with this vision that Dante closed *The Divine Comedy*:

> I raised my eyes aloft, and I beheld
> The scattered chapters of the Universe
> Gathered and bound into a single book
> By the austere and tender hand of God.

It is that "austere and tender hand of God" which makes the tiger and the lamb dwell together in Christians. He makes our gentleness strong, and he tempers our austerity with love.

IX

PRUDENCE AND CARELESSNESS

For which of you, desiring to build a tower, doth not first sit down and count the cost? —Luke 14:28
Be not therefore anxious for the morrow. —Matt. 6:34

To TAKE THESE TWO TEXTS OUT OF THEIR CONTEXT AND PUT THEM IN contrast to one another seems to make the gospel utterly contradictory. In the one place it seems that Jesus is counseling an almost exaggerated prudence on the part of his followers. They are not to begin anything until they have counted the complete cost and are sure they can finish what they have started. Yet in the Sermon on the Mount Jesus seems to be saying that it is wrong to take into consideration all the possibilities of the morrow. We are to trust that everything will go well and leave it at that. The outsider may wonder what Jesus really means. Is the Christian one who practices prudence, or is he one who is utterly careless about the future?

The answer to the seeming contradiction of these two questions is that in some ways the Christian is to be more prudent than other men, and in other ways he is to be more careless than other men. Concerning some matters he will impress his contemporaries as being of such careful habits that they will regard him as foolish. But in other fields, which the world considers with greatest prudence, the Christian will show a casual carelessness.

CHRISTIAN PRUDENCE

The Christian's deep concern for certain values in life always remains a mystery to the non-Christian. The Christian seems to see

98

dangers where others see none at all. He is accused by many of making mountains out of molehills. He is aware of tendencies which must be fought and destroyed before they gain power. He is always seeing on the horizon a cloud no bigger than a man's hand which to him foretells a coming storm.

Whenever anything threatens the dignity of human life, the Christian is profoundly troubled. He is so sensitive to the rights of every man that the slightest hint of their abrogation arouses in him a resentment and an opposition. When Mary Wollstonecraft published her *Vindication of the Rights of Women* in 1792, Hannah More, a novelist of the period, commented: "Rights of Women! We will be hearing of the Rights of Children next!" The deep concern of the Christian for the rights of all human creatures is something which others find terribly difficult to comprehend. Instead of finding sympathy for his concern the Christian learns to expect an irritated impatience.

There is a tendency among men of little faith to be willing to trade freedom for comfort. They are not aware of what is involved in this transaction, and it always seems to them worth giving up a few rights for protection and security. In fact the encroachment of security on freedom is hardly apparent to most men. But it is apparent to the Christian, and he opposes it with all his might. He knows how quickly tyranny grows and how suddenly its seeming harmlessness becomes dangerous. Men have a terrible tendency to awaken too late to the threat of antihuman forces. But by his faith the Christian is made extra sensitive to the danger of these threats. He is grounded in the doctrine that men, because of what they are, must be free. This is an essential human need for which no substitute can be found. The Christian, therefore, shouts his warning and is usually regarded as a fool for his pains.

The Christian is most prudent when it comes to respecting the inner life of man. The materialist is always worried about things that show, but the Christian is concerned primarily about the things within, for it is there that the real issues must be decided. Christianity has a deep belief that the soul is immortal, and any damage to the soul is an eternal damage. That is why attitudes of hatred and hardness and revenge are regarded with such seriousness by Jesus and warned against by Christian teachers. Inner attitudes are more significant than outward acts of violence. The deep concern for things which cannot be seen is often regarded as exaggerated prudence.

The Christian is always sensitive to compromise because he knows that in the plea for a reasonable compromise there is the danger of losing the real value. He opposes the doctrine that the end justifies the means. He knows that the means which are used to attain any goal will have their effect upon the goal itself and certainly upon the men who use them. This Christian concern and prudence, which is exercised in relationship to all that affects the dignity of men and the inner life of men, gives to many critics of the gospel the impression of an unhealthy carefulness.

How many times in recent days, for example, have the militarists felt that the tender consciences of Christian people were ridiculous and morbid. In time of war how impatient so-called practical men are with the protests of Christians. In the hysteria generated by the nation's war effort it seems to many people that nothing matters except the marshaling of all the human resources for military victory. Let human dignity wait! Let conscience be set aside as a luxury we cannot now afford! Why make an effort to honor the individual's rights in a crisis, even if they are guaranteed by the Constitution? The Christian will insist on maintaining the tension of the inviolability of human dignity, even in times of greatest stress. He knows that every denial of that dignity makes it easier the next time, and that under the claim of a perpetual crisis the denial can be made complete and permanent. As de Toqueville said in 1835, a democratic people will find it difficult to start a war and just as difficult to end it. What damage has been wrought to democracy in the name of emergency! How hard it is to get rid of totalitarian practices, even when the special situation is ended! This is why the

Church so often fights a battle against an enemy not visible to secularists.

John Huss was brought before a church council willing to acquit him if he would but yield his insistence on individual freedom. One of the cardinals went so far as to advise his submitting to the council, warning him if he refused to do so, his security and even his life would be in danger. To none of these arguments would the brave martyr yield. Instead he sent a letter to his friends in Bohemia, saying: "I write this in prison and in chains, expecting tomorrow to receive a sentence of death, full of hope in God that I shall not swerve from the truth, nor abjure errors imputed to me by false witnesses. . . . In the truth which I have proclaimed, according to the gospel of Jesus Christ, . . . I will, this day, joyfully die." And there it is—an extreme prudence in speaking the truth, and yet utter carelessness so far as saving his own life was concerned. This seems to be a complete reversal of common sense.

PRUDENCE AND TOMORROW

Jesus' picture of the unfinished tower and the builder's embarrassment because of his failure has a number of implications. Certainly it is warning us not to count on an introductory enthusiasm to finish the job. The discipleship to which we are called is difficult and exacting, and it is for life. It will take more than a burst of emotion. It is all right to talk about the low aim being crime, but high aim without corresponding ability is not ennobling—it is only futile. The abortive efforts of well-meaning but unsteadfast idealists does the cause of goodness much harm. If the Christian is careless about tomorrow's unpredictables, he has a prudent concern for the adequacy of his own resources.

The Bible brings this constantly to the attention of men. It urges us to seek the Lord in the days of our youth. It tells us how uncertain a day may be. It commands us to hold our actions under the discipline of the Holy Spirit and to be spiritually prepared. The Bible knows how very bitter the old age of the wicked can be and describes its horror. It knows also how very beautiful is the old age of the saint. It is frankly frightened at the future of a man who has drifted away from righteousness. It urges an extreme prudence in making present decisions, because it knows the future sadness which evil has in store for us.

This prudence in regard to the investment of our talents and our time is due also to the realization of how short life is at best. Disraeli once said, "Life is too short to be little." While some men may say that it is justifiable to kill time and one has a right to make his own decisions since his life is his own, the Christian is aware that time is not to be squandered and his life is not his own. His life belongs to God and to the service of his brethren. He must exercise, therefore, a careful prudence in the use of the minutes which are entrusted to him.

A man should be deeply aware of the uncertainty of life. He lives in a world of danger, and there is always the possibility of accident. He knows he has no guarantee that disaster will not come to him as well as to other men. The real Christian knows that God's plan to create great character and free persons demanded a world in which there should be risk and uncertainty. While others, therefore, may condone the sowing of wild oats and the enjoyment of life in cheap and trivial ways, the Christian cannot bring himself to believe that this is wisdom. He leans over backward in taking his life seriously and investing it carefully. Every passing moment is of such precious significance he cannot bring himself to waste one of them. His own gifts, he knows, are but loaned to him by his heavenly Father. He is a steward of God responsible for the use of his talents. He cannot escape by burying his talent, and the time will arrive when he must give an account of every wasted moment and every murdered hour.

It is interesting to note that modern psychology has vindicated Christianity's concern for time so far as the education of children is concerned. It is not true that nothing important takes place in the early years. Quite the contrary! Infancy is the time when matters of utmost importance are decided. It is then that millstones are hung around the necks of little ones. During that crucial period life finds its wings. How precious are the passing seconds of childhood! The Christian never says there is plenty of time and he can start later on. He cannot feel there is no need for hurry in making the best use of his own life in the present moment. In the matter of the investment of his time and in the business of sowing today what he would like to reap tomorrow the Christian exercises a prudence that often seems extreme to his less serious brother.

Yet a Divine Carelessness

But on the other hand we discover that the Christian has only contempt for what the pagan takes very seriously. If he is overly prudent in one realm of life, he seems to be overly careless in another. As Halford Luccock said, he has learned that "posterity is a perverse mistress to work for. She rarely pays any attention to what was written especially for her, but she is often curious about what was written in supreme unconcern for her." [1] The Christian has very little concern for what have been called the treasures of earth. He remembers the word of his Lord that it is better to lay up treasures in heaven, where moth and rust doth not corrupt and where thieves cannot break in and steal. The materialist has little concern about treasures in heaven, but he wants treasures on earth.

When a well-known movie star, who had gained all the world has to give, committed suicide, a news magazine commented on the tragic affair and gave a brief account of her life. It pointed out that she had attained what most American girls think they would like to have. By using her beauty and her glamour she married several men who could further her ambitions. She used and then discarded her husbands when she was weary of them, or they could no longer serve her. All the tawdriness and tragedy of our life was summed up in her career. All the cheapness of the treasures in which we put our trust was revealed in her poor life. We cannot read her story without remembering the words of Jesus, "What shall it profit a man, if he shall gain the whole world, and lose his own soul?"

[1] *In the Minister's Workshop* (New York and Nashville: Abingdon-Cokesbury Press, 1946), p. 54.

(K.J.V.) Too many sell their souls and give their lives to attain such questionable distinction. The Christian understands that in the pursuit of earthly honor a divine kind of carelessness is wisdom. Too many worldly treasures demand too high a price. To the world the Christian asks Isaiah's question: "Wherefore do ye spend money for that which is not bread? and your labour for that which satisfieth not?" (Isa. 55:2.)

This failure to give lasting satisfaction is in the Christian's judgment true of what we call success. He cannot get excited about giving his life to the pursuit of passing thrills. There falls upon him a disillusionment concerning the whole mad enterprise, and at last he turns careless eyes upon it. Success worshipers wonder at his impracticality and his otherworldliness. So many things society does with such intensity in an effort to find amusement leave the Christian unmoved. He cannot see that they are very much fun. He cannot be convinced that, even if he should attain those so-called values, he would find any pleasure in them. Thoreau one time said that a man is rich in proportion to the number of things he can get along without. The Christian discovers that, so far as these earthly trinkets are concerned, he can get along without a great many of them. He finds, indeed, that he is better off without them, and certainly a life dedicated to their pursuit seems to him to be a life wasted.

When one looks at the places of amusement in our modern society, he is alarmed, not so much by their wickedness as by their tawdriness. Can it be that people actually get into such a condition that they enjoy night clubs and the vulgar exhibitions of café society? Some people are never able to understand that others can despise the thing they value so highly. It is so often true that individuals come to look upon Christians as peculiar people because they have only contempt for that which the world worships.

PRUDENT CARELESSNESS

There is created in the Christian's character a prudent carelessness or a careless prudence, whichever you may prefer. It is always out of step with the wisdom of the world and has about it an "Alice in Wonderland" quality. That is to say, it often appears to the practical man as a kind of madness. The clue to its nature is in the Christian doctrines of the nature of man and the life everlasting. The world approaches the problem of values by assuming that it is more important to have than to be and that every policy is to be based on the assumption that men are creatures of this earth only. Christians believe that they have immortal souls and the quality of their characters is much more important than the abundance of their possessions. Thus, according to the world's standards, prudence and carelessness get reversed.

One of the greatest dangers good men face is becoming too careful about minor affairs. It is possible to practice a giant concern for a pigmy matter. One time the clerk of a very eminent trader came to Dr. Samuel Johnson and confessed what he thought was a very serious fault. He said he had been tempted from time to time to take paper and packthread from his employer for his own use, and indeed he had done so. Johnson suggested that in all probability the master would not take this too seriously if the clerk should go and confess his sin. The clerk said he had already confessed, and the master had dismissed it as of no importance whatsoever. Johnson then inquired of his visitor at what hour he had left the counting house and at what hour he went to bed. When he learned the answers to these questions, he said in his devastating way, "Then I have at least learned thus much by my new acquaintance;—that five hours of the four-and-twenty unemployed are enough for a man to go mad in; so I would advise you, Sir, to study algebra, if you are not an adept already in it: your head would get less muddy, and you would leave off tormenting your neighbours about paper and packthread, while we all live together in a world that is bursting with sin and sorrow." A healthy Christian conscience makes a man aware that sin and sorrow are more important than paper and thread.

The prudent carelessness of the gospel is a cure for the anxiety of men. For while it makes them extremely careful about a good many things for which they are to blame and for which they are responsible, it makes them utterly free of worry concerning the things which they cannot affect. Anxiety is often caused by worry over things which are beyond our control anyway. For this the Christian has no concern. He lives in what Dale Carnegie has called "day-tight compartments." "Sufficient unto the day is the evil thereof," he believes. "Be not therefore anxious for the morrow" is the guiding rule of his life. But about the things which really matter to his spirit he is concerned and he is prudent, because they spell life or death for him.

It is this prudent carelessness that gives us freedom and helps us to live without fear. It makes us understand the things which we can do and the things we ought to do. It makes us able to see the things that are not important and the matters in which we should be ashamed to be engaged. The gospel tells men that about some things they ought to be more prudent than they have been and more prudent than their neighbors are willing to be. But about the serious pursuit of objects whose attainment results in disappointment anyway they are to be unconcerned and careless. This gives Christians one of the most engaging qualities, namely, a gallant and independent integrity.

The great scientist Thomas Huxley one time gave this description of his idea of God: "The player on the other side is hidden from us. We know that his play is always fair, just, and patient. But also we know, to our cost, that he never overlooks a mistake, or makes the smallest allowance for ignorance. To the man who plays well, the highest stakes are paid, with that sort of overflowing generosity with which the strong shows delight in strength. And one who plays ill is checkmated—without haste, but without remorse." This is not the Christian idea of God, yet the Christian too is aware of the game which must be played fairly, justly, and patiently. It must be played with prudence. But because the judge of the game is like a heavenly Father who forgives and who loves, it can also be played without fear and with perfect trust.

Quiller-Couch said of John Wesley: "One secret of his power was that he always spoke with authority and another was his kingly neglect of trifles, for he paid no heed to the signs which made his hearers judge of themselves and others as lost beyond recovery." This authority and neglect of trifles is the secret of the Christian's poise. There is no greater depression than when the seemingly exciting quality of sin turns into dullness and weariness. Nor is there any enterprise more satisfying than the pursuit of a goodness whose fascination increases the closer we approach it. When the gospel has its chance with us, it reveals that a serious pursuit of evil is silly, and we turn aside from it with a wonderful carelessness. But by opening our eyes to the achievements worthy of men with eternal destinies, the gospel makes us prudent in the realms which God deems significant. Thus we can "first sit down and count the cost" and at the same time "be not anxious for the morrow."

X

HUMILITY AND ASSURANCE

But the publican . . . smote his breast, saying, God, be thou merciful to me a sinner.   —Luke 18:13

For I reckon that I am not a whit behind the very chiefest apostles.   —II Cor. 11:5

HUMILITY IS PROBABLY THE MOST UNPOPULAR VIRTUE DEMANDED BY the gospel. At least it is unpopular when it comes to practicing it in our own lives, though we are sorry to note its absence in the lives of others. Perhaps it is this difficulty of practice that encouraged the Nazis to make a virtue out of pride. How often do we note that men try to justify their weaknesses and minimize the virtues which are not easy to enjoy. It is this frame of mind which made Nietzsche refer to Christianity as a kind of slave morality.

Yet strangely enough, until a man knows humility he cannot have assurance. These two elements, oftentimes regarded as opposites, are in reality necessary to each other. The kind of assurance which does not rest on true humility is a very unstable thing and does not last very long. It is primarily pretense. But when men dare to be humble, then they receive, strangely enough, an assurance that nothing can overcome. It is the Christian gospel which brings these two things together in a tension and a balance.

PRIDE

According to religious insight, the fundamental sin of life is pride, for it is pride which is the breaking of the First Commandment. Human pride is an anti-God state of mind from which spring all the other sins. The Jews had a clear insight when they said the First Commandment was that men should worship one God and refuse to share that loyalty with other gods or values. When, therefore, a man regards himself as an equal with God and in his pride thinks more highly of himself than he ought to think, he is guilty of an ultimate irreverence.

A generation that knows its Bible can never forget this lesson. But a biblically ignorant generation, such as ours, too often forgets it. This is the meaning of the story of the Garden of Eden in the book of Genesis. However we may differ in our attitudes toward that story, or however we may regard it, the essential thing we are supposed to learn from it is that when men try to usurp the place of God, they are driven forth to judgment. When the serpent promised Adam and Eve they would "be as gods," he was tempting them to strive for something men must not desire. He was guilty also of the greatest grammatical sin, which is to make plural what can be only singular. Woe unto men when they forget there can never be "gods" but only God! That ancient story is repeated over and over again in the lives of individuals and in the histories of nations.

According to the prophetic interpretation of history, it was pride that led nations to destruction. The prophets never believed that defeat was merely a matter of might against weakness. It was always a matter of right against wrong. When things went well, it meant that a nation was loyal to God. Whenever things began to go wrong, the prophets traced the cause to the pride of Israel's political rulers and to the corruption within the nation. With almost monotonous regularity in certain Old Testament books there occur concerning one after another of Israel's kings the words, "He walked in the way of his fathers." Which is to say that he denied God and put himself too high.

In the teaching of Jesus this thought is underlying, and he illustrates it from many angles. Even the story of the prodigal son in the gospel of Luke has the evil of pride for one of its minor themes. The elder brother was guilty of the assumption that he deserved more from his father than the younger boy who had gone astray.

Whatever else we want to make of the boy who stayed at home, we cannot escape the implication in the thinking of Jesus that pride made him a worse sinner than his brother, in spite of his obvious moral superiority. The teaching of our Lord insists that until a man is humble, no good thing can come from him, no matter what he may do.

Let us remember Paul's great word concerning Jesus, "He humbled himself." That which the Master had demanded of others he demanded first of himself. He had implied many times that the servant is not greater than his lord. When the Lord of heaven himself came down to earth to humble himself before sinners, that was the ultimate proclamation of the necessity for humility. Paul needed this example, and so does every man. How easy it is for us to have pride in our own accomplishments. How easily Paul could have been the great egotist of the Christian movement. Yet his pride is held in check, and his powerful drives are controlled by the spirit of Jesus Christ, who was the perfect example of humility.

We shall not say this Christian virtue is commanded because it is something special for Christians. It is commanded because life demands it. The story of all human endeavor is that pride goeth before a fall. It takes us long to learn this truth, and usually we don't learn it until too late. Certain it is that the farther away a man or a people get from Jesus Christ, the less check they have upon this human tendency to be proud. One of the greatest contributions of the gospel to men is to keep them aware that they are men and not gods.

Our whole way of life tends to encourage pride. It is not true that men are so foolish as to think that money, beyond a certain amount, is valuable in itself. But they are tempted under our system of individualism and free enterprise to impress the neighbors with their success. We are in danger of going to any extreme necessary to increase our prestige. It gives us too much satisfaction to be above others economically and socially. It is easy to drift far from Jesus' principle that a man is great in terms of his service and not because of his possessions. When we lust for a place above our brethren, we can hardly regard them as anything more than means to an end. Unfortunately, pride is a universal evil and the fundamental weakness in us all. It takes more than will power to keep modesty's gestures from veiling the motives of pride.

HUMILITY

Over and against this evil the gospel puts the virtue of humility. It understands that greatness is always humble. The truly great, for the most part, have little time to spend looking great or acting great. One of the most interesting things about leaders is that so seldom do they consciously play the part. Some French journalists one time visited the House of Commons in London and heard two socialists speak. They were perfectly attired in the best clothes of the latest fashion. A little later Lord Robert Cecil arose to speak, but he was dressed casually, almost carelessly. At best, he had never been a triumph for his tailor. "Ah," said one of the Frenchmen, "at last here is a true worker." It is usually the case that the real aristocrat wears his breeding with a casual grace, while the man who is not quite sure of his eminence goes to any length in order to impress his contemporaries. For genuineness can afford humility, while the pretender must depend on surface glitter.

The man who knows how to be humble is the man who finds the truth. It is here that Christianity and science come close together. Jesus' word, "Except ye . . . become as little children, ye shall in no wise enter into the kingdom of heaven," is understood by every great scientist. Science always goes wrong when it begins to be proud of its humility. It always goes wrong when it begins to talk about the creeds it imagines it has destroyed. The great temptation of the scientist is to go beyond his field and become a philosopher. Then it is easy for him to be as dogmatic and unscientific as a fundamentalist. We have at last awakened to the realization that an arrogant scientist is a denial of his profession. We have grown aware increasingly that a generation in bondage to a narrow scientism is no better off than if it were bound by a narrow theology. One of the greatest statements about this whole matter was made by

Thomas Huxley in a letter to Charles Kingsley. In reply to a letter Kingsley had written on the death of Huxley's son he wrote: "Science seems to me to teach in the highest and strongest manner the great truth which is embodied in the Christian conception of entire surrender to the will of God. Sit down before fact as a little child, be prepared to give up every preconceived notion, follow humbly wherever and to whatever abysses Nature leads, or you shall learn nothing. I have only begun to learn content and peace of mind since I have resolved at all risks to do this." Only thus do we learn the truth. The humble man is willing to learn from anyone, and because of that willingness, he does learn from anyone. Woe unto the man who is afraid to step aside for another man! He has doomed himself to stand forever in his own light. This is not to say that we must assume that every man who pushes us aside is right. But while he reveals himself, we shall learn much for our profit.

This virtue of humility brings true happiness. It alone can take us from the defensive and make us feel safe. It is a cure for our inferiority complex and also for our superiority complex. It protects us from always being hurt by what we fancy are slights from other people. It makes it unnecessary for us to maintain some fancied high position and insist that other people shall always recognize that position. It takes the strain from us and brings us peace. It is amazing what a friendly, decent place the world is when a man has rid himself of his pride.

One of those wise fools who had observed a half-truth and blown it up as an explanation of all the world's troubles had the theory that all our difficulty is due to the construction of buildings more than one story high. "As a matter of fact," he would say, "a house should normally be made to shelter men. It is not natural to add stories to it. For in falling from the fifth floor, for instance, you kill yourself. But that would be nothing. What is serious is that the invention of stories has made large cities possible. Large cities have made possible the formation of masses. With the masses have arisen the great social problems. And these are at the origin of the wars of the twentieth century. The whole evil arises from houses with more than one story." [1] To most of us this will seem like an oversimplification. But that most of our troubles arise from building our own egos too high is simply a sober judgment. The vaulting ambition which raises us above other men in our own eyes is like building a skyscraper on faulty foundations. It becomes a death trap, and its fascination is fatal.

A proud and successful people have a tendency to think they are right even when they are wrong. People ought to be a little fearful that they are wrong even when they are right. The future belongs to those who are sensitive and responsive to criticism, and the future always belongs to the men who are not afraid to believe they can be wrong and sometimes are. Not only the future but the present belongs to them also. They are happy men. They are at home in the world. This is one of the fundamental lessons which the gospel teaches us. The Lord can do such great things for us if we are humble, and so very little for us when we are proud.

Assurance

Yet out of this humility there comes a great assurance. The humble person is not what you sometimes expect him to be. He is not a doormat upon which you can walk. He is not a neutral, negative character who counts for nothing. He is a man who is relaxed, and he has a quiet, underlying confidence which disturbs the self-assured. We must understand first that this humility is not a negative characteristic at all, but a very positive and satisfying one.

So much of our pretended superiority is really insecurity. It is a camouflage to cover up something we must hide. Sometimes it is an escape from ourselves, and oftentimes it is merely a fear to look at what we really are. That the so-called superiority complex is very often the defense of a man who knows anxiety in his own heart has been pointed out so many times it has become trite. I think that in the vast majority of cases the man who boasts too much about his own accomplishments and his own gifts is really a man who is very unsure about their validity.

[1] Denis de Rougemont, *The Devil's Share* (New York: Pantheon Press, 1944), p. 151.

This is true of an arrogant society. A great people, assured of their own power and of their own values, do not have to go around constantly threatening their neighbors. A legitimate nationalism, therefore, is always humble and willing to learn from others. True nationalism always respects the rights of others and the accomplishments of others. It is never too proud to listen to smaller nations. Arrogant boasting, which has been so characteristic of our time, has not been primarily a sign of real strength, but merely an indication of an insecure nation with memories of past humiliations, trying to play the part of a tough bully.

Whenever we go on the defensive against the race question or a civil rights program, it is not because we are powerful and assured. It is because in American life we cannot deny civil rights to any person without feeling guilty about it. Thus we have to lean over backward and challenge every suggested righting of the injustice. If only men could recognize humbly their own guilt as the reason for their fear of justice, something might be done to attack the problems of injustice. There would come then a quiet assurance that the problem can be solved in such a way that everyone will gain from the solution. Unfortunately there are so few people who have been touched with Christian humility.

The Old Testament incident of the tower of Babel is more than an entertaining story. When men forget that they are of the earth, they are visited with confusion. To assume we have the power in ourselves to storm the gates of heaven is blasphemy. Of what value is material progress when it destroys our unity and makes us unable to understand one another? Then all the implements we took pride in as aids to more rapid progress turn out to be dangerous trinkets helping us toward a more speedy destruction. Then it is that the vision of the brave new world turns into a nightmare of black night, slaughter, and death.

The danger of Communism in our time is a strange kind of danger with which we hardly know how to cope. The truth is that Communism challenges us at our own weak points. Communism has moved in where there has been a vacuum, or wherever there has been a denial of democratic doctrine. It is an alert foe probing our hypocrisy. The real defense, therefore, is a humility which freely admits our failures and then shows a desire to do something about them. Communism, in a sense, stands over against democracy like a conscience, pointing out and exaggerating any weaknesses that may be in it. A victory for democracy over Communism must be moral and spiritual rather than military.

Christian humility is nothing like defeat. There is a vast difference between pagan humility and Christian humility. When the pride of the pagan is broken, he has nothing left. Then he has to weep and wail, as did Ecclesiastes, and in the words of that pessimistic book he says: "All things are full of weariness; man cannot utter it: the eye is not satisfied with seeing, nor the ear filled with hearing. That which hath been is that which shall be; and that which hath been done is that which shall be done: and there is no new thing under the sun." (1:8-9.) It is the knowledge that if his pride is taken from him he has no other resources left which makes the pagan hang onto it with such tenacity. The Christian is in a quite different situation.

Before God can do his work, the Christian must know his own inadequacy and confess it to God. Yet this is an experience which does not weaken him, but it re-creates him. It makes him able at last to deal with the little, annoying things which are, after all, the destructive things in life. In George Santayana's novel *The Last Puritan* one of the characters says:

Ah, the little troubles, Mr. Oliver, they ruin a woman's life. It's the devil, I do believe, as sends us the toothache and the east wind. . . . As for your grand sorrows, they are a parcel of our common humanity, like funerals; and the Lord designs them for our good, to wean our hearts from this sad world. There's where the Vicar can comfort me, where I don't need comforting; and it's almost a pleasure to grieve, all hung in weeds, like a weeping willow. But the price of eggs, Mr. Oliver, the price of eggs! [2]

[2] (New York: Charles Scribner's Sons, 1936), p. 276.

The proud man is destroyed by the little things. But the humble man will take those little annoyances with a new patience and be saved from their corrupting power.

Proud Humility

There is created for the Christian this strange contradiction—a humble assurance, a proud humility. The Christian is a haughtier man, in a sense, than was ever known before, because he is so sure of eternity and of God. He will not be pushed aside as if he were of no worth. Like Paul, he will take his place beside the chief apostles, for he knows that is where he belongs. He does no more wailing about the brutishness of human life or the terrible remark of Homer's that a man is the saddest of all the beasts of the field. No more of that! Yet, because he is a son of God and falls far short of being worthy of that heritage, the Christian is the chief of sinners, and he knows it. So at the same time he experiences the most far-reaching humility.

It is the willingness to see each man in the light of this paradox and to recognize one's own life in this light that makes a Christian society possible. J. E. L. Newbigin, bishop of Madara, South India, remarked that when he came back from India, he was impressed by seeing lines of people waiting for a London bus. Nobody tried to get in front of the others; nobody thought that because he had more money he should get on first. Each man assumed that he must take his place in line and wait until his turn came, whoever the men ahead of him might be. This kind of thing, which we accept so easily, is really part of the Christian gospel's molding of life, and it is a part of its creativeness. Precisely because we have this deep assurance, we know that other men must be treated as equals, and with humility we take our place with them and ask no favors over them.

This is a great miracle of the gospel. It unites humility and assurance in a new combination. This is the new creature in Jesus Christ. It is not easy to maintain the balance, as any man knows. We have no other way except to be constantly immersing ourselves in the spirit of Christ. Then are we able to stand before Pilate, and

116

when he says, "Are you a king?" we answer, "Thou sayest it." At the same time it is possible for us to kneel before our brethren with a towel and a basin of water, washing their feet in the spirit of service and humility. In the Christian life humbleness and assurance find their true relationships and their true balance.

When Lord Bryce, author of that classic study *The American Commonwealth*, came to this country to work with Professor Macy of Grinnell University, he stayed with his collaborator for several weeks. The Macy household had no servants except a part-time cook, but the Englishman, on the basis of his experience in English country houses, assumed that there would be someone about to shine his shoes if he left them outside his door at night. Macy took the shoes each night and shined them himself, and the distinguished British statesman and scholar never knew that his host had also been his servant. So is our relationship with our Lord. He lived among men as a servant, and he shamed their petty desires for prominence. With our eyes on his example we cannot feel that we have ever known real humiliation, and strangely enough, because he has made us aware of the dignity of our sonship, the annoying hurts and ignorings have no effect on us. We are redeemed from many a petty irritation that formerly made us angry and ashamed. Once we can cry out sincerely, "God, be thou merciful to me a sinner!" he sends us to our tasks with the assurance that we are not a whit behind the very chiefest apostles.

XI

CONTEMPORARY AND TIMELESS

Today is salvation come to this house.   —Luke 19:9
Jesus Christ is the same yesterday and today, yea and for ever.
                                                —Heb. 13:8

No man thinks very long about the problems of life without coming to the problem of time. This matter, which on the surface seems to be so simple as to be scarcely worth a second thought, proves to have within it all the mysteries of life itself. Many philosophers have not been satisfied to regard time as a river flowing between rigid banks. On the contrary, they have considered it as another dimension of a great eternal present. What, they have asked, does time look like? A first-rate scientist came to the conclusion that man in his dreams moves backward and forward from present to future to past, even as he can move backward and forward in space. If he is not capable of going into the complexities of the problem, at least each man knows that he must deal with things which are timeless, as well as things which are only contemporary.

For the Christian the problem is a real one because he knows himself to be a creature of both time and eternity. He has a sense of the significance of the passing moments, and he also has a sense of the littleness of his own experience. He is conscious of how time destroys nearly everything that man builds. Just as the psalmist suggested, he too is aware of man as grass which lasts but a little while. Yet he finds himself plunged into eternity and in the midst of values which will be real and true a thousand years from now. He feels that he is the weakest of the creatures of the earth and in

118

some ways the most pitiful because of the brief moment he has. But he also feels himself to be older than the mountains and to have a destiny that will outlast the stars.

How does a man adjust himself creatively to this contemporary and timeless feeling? How can he treat the passing moments with proper respect when he knows that eternity is his? Yet how can he keep his mind centered on eternity when all around him there is the change and the decay which he cannot overlook? He finds his best answer in the gospel. Its view and experience make a man able to cope with the problem of time. For the gospel sets everything, including man, in a proper perspective.

The Bible moves back and forth between the poles of man's apparent transitoriness and his everlasting value. Just when it seems to be overwhelmed with the sadness of his brief existence, it gives a shout of triumph as a new vision of his indestructibility falls upon it. The Scriptures do not deny the temporary qualities in human life, which make pessimists of so many philosophers. But they have a sense of time which is not confined to the temporary and hence is not at the mercy of pessimism. Time for the Christian becomes a friendly servant instead of a cruel master. For too many people it is the other way around.

CAPTURED BY THE PAST

For one thing, men are oftentimes too enamored with the past, and it has too great an influence on their thinking. It is too influential in determining their sense of values. We see it in the ancestor worship associated with certain religions. It is not true that ancestor worship is only an idolatry of yesterday. It is still with us, and it is still very vital. More significant in the minds of some people than any present accomplishment by their own efforts is the fact that they are descended from great men of the generations gone. It is probably true that the worst discovery that has been made by some individuals is the notable accomplishments of their great-grandfathers. If only they could be cut loose from that tyranny and realize that any claim to greatness must depend upon their own

119

activity and their own character, they might accomplish something worth while. The past has been to them an enslavement.

That is true of some organizations which regard themselves as the descendants and heirs of the great revolutionaries of this country. One of the most amusing things in the contemporary scene, if it were not so tragic in its implications, is to see how these descendants of radicals have become in their own time the reactionaries. If something of the revolutionary spirit of their fathers had been passed on to them, so that they were pioneers in this day as their ancestors were in theirs, then there would be something noble and inspiring about remembering those great men. But when they deny the very values for which their fathers stood, they show themselves to be the true descendants of the Tories, not the Revolutionists. They reveal how little they understand the past and how the past is betrayed.

It is possible for the present to become the captive of the past. Yesterday sometimes comes to be a chain around today's efforts. To respect yesterday and yet not be enslaved by it is one of the difficult tasks which we are called upon to perform. It is too easy to pay lip service to past sacrifices and then make those gallant deaths meaningless by our behavior. How quickly the high aims for which a war is fought are forgotten by the common man! It is hardly over before the same old selfish scheming is under way, and the same old selfish pursuits are accepted. Memorial Day comes, and we make our speeches and preach our sermons about how grateful we are to the young men who died, and then go out to desecrate their deaths by making them of no avail. Perhaps if the world had the power to understand that it is the trustee of a million deaths, it would not so easily commit the blasphemy of denying the principles for which the young men died. The evil of the past is too often a stronger influence on the present than those who gave their lives to set us free from it.

The story of institutions is very often a story of their inability to choose the present over the past. Religious institutions particularly have shown themselves, in generation after generation, as examples of Jesus' warning that you cannot put new wine into old wine sacks. Judaism in his day was the living example of that observation. I have been able to find no indication that Jesus came to found a new religion deliberately. He would have been quite content to reform the faith of his own people. He came not to destroy but to fulfill. It was Judaism's fascination for yesterday which kept it from accepting the promise Jesus brought for the present and the future. Christianity was born when Judaism showed its preference for yesterday over today.

The story was repeated again within the Christian Church when the Reformation became a reality. There is no sign in the beginning that Martin Luther, for example, consciously planned a new church. There are many indications that his hope was to reform the Church from within. He did not wish to move out from it and set up a rival institution. He was forced out when those in places of power thought they might get through the crisis without reformation. Protestantism would have been unnecessary if Roman Catholicism had given up its inordinate respect for the dead hand of the past.

It is a human tendency to regard something as completely accomplished and hence to be considered as a finality. Benjamin Rush of Philadelphia, in his *Address to the People of the United States*, said something that was not only true of the Revolution, but of many another movement:

There is nothing more common than to confound the terms of the American Revolution with those of the late American war. The American war is over: but this is far from being the case with the American Revolution. On the contrary, nothing but the first act of the great drama is closed. It remains yet to establish and perfect our new forms of government; and to prepare the principles, morals, and manners of our citizens, for these forms of government, after they are established and brought to perfection.

If individuals and institutions alike had some understanding of the unfinished tasks bequeathed to the present by the past, they could then see the past in its true meaning. It would become not a prison but an inspiration.

Let the Christian remember Jesus' command to let the dead bury the dead. His message was one of release from the bad habits and the mistakes of the past. He came to remove the burdens of guilt by forgiving sin and thus giving men another chance. Long before modern psychology revealed the terrifying burdens bequeathed to men from their forgotten years, Jesus understood and lifted those burdens. Whatever else the Christian doctrine of forgiveness means, it is release from the chains forged by previous sin.

No one understood this more clearly than Paul. We are impressed now with his successes, but he must have been impressed with his failures and disappointments. One of the wonderful things about the Apostle to the Gentiles was his ability to carry the terrible burdens of frustration and betrayal without breaking under them. What kept him from having a nervous breakdown? How did he keep his health? Where did his courage come from, and how could he do the impossible? One of the main clues to these questions is given in his words "forgetting the things which are behind." One of the greatest gifts of our Lord is the power to remain uncaptured by the past.

To Despise the Past

The other extreme is that men do not take the past seriously enough. They do not understand the true nature of progress. They assume that today can be independent of what has already happened. They rush in to give too much credit to the man who is standing upon the shoulders of numerous men who have gone before him. They lose sight of the continuity of human life and human progress. Like Marcion's second-century heresy which advocated eliminating the Old Testament from Christianity's Bible, these people would believe that things come full-grown and have no vital connection with the old.

A nineteenth-century thinker said, "The historian is a prophet looking backwards." This man saw clearly that the past is prophetic of the future. If a historian is something more than just a gatherer of dead facts, he will become a prophet for the present because he has a true understanding of the past. Certainly the Hebrew prophet was a man who learned from yesterday and proclaimed those lessons to his own generation. We have not truly understood the significance of yesterday until we see it as the prophet sees it—a living prelude to the present.

To despise the past is to create within society a rootlessness, which is one of the saddest characteristics of our time. A drifting people without any sense of the long traditions which are theirs are a people without stamina enough to withstand disaster and defeat. Tradition is not necessarily that which binds us to something gone and keeps us from living in the present. It is, in reality, an agreement with yesterday. When we come to understand our tradition, we see that we have an obligation to our fathers and are a part of something that was here long before we arrived. A tradition is a stabilizer and a messenger from eternity.

Civilization always needs this sense of continuity, and without it there is no lasting culture possible. Just as there is a vast difference between old established families and the *nouveaux riche*, so there is a vast difference between a people who think that everything worth while is their own creation and the people who know their roots go far back into the past. When the crisis has arrived and a people must make their choice, they will certainly be deeply affected either by a sense of their history or by the lack of it. If they do not know all that has gone into the creation of their ideals and the painful sacrifices made by their fathers, they will find it much easier to betray those ideals and surrender them. It is true, therefore, that while yesterday can become an enslaving force, it can also become an inspiring and strengthening power.

Many a man who stands on the rim of the Grand Canyon of the Colorado feels something stir within him that he has never felt before. If he is disappointed with that view, I think there is nothing on the face of the earth that will not be a disappointment to him. It is the world's supreme example of erosion. It has taken seven or eight million years to create that wonder of nature. But as J. B.

Priestley, the English novelist, remarked, one has the feeling when he is there that God gave the Colorado River its instruction.[1] One who looks into that miracle can never believe that everything began with him, or that everything that went on before his coming was insignificant. So when the past is truly understood and respected, it becomes an inspiration and a steadying influence. It is a good thing to feel a sense of obligation to God and the men who bequeathed unto us our goodly heritage.

To Despise the Present

Now when a man comes to take the eternal point of view, which is the gospel's point of view, he faces the danger of despising the present, or at least of not taking the present seriously enough. He may look at today with an unmoved will. He may say that, after all, nothing matters very much if you look at it from the long point of view. It will be all the same in another hundred years. The man who takes this attitude then loses the realization that the time for decision is now. He loses the sense of moments with all the significance of a thousand years in them. He cannot comprehend that his decision just at this moment may have for himself and for his fellows many and varied consequences which will not end even with his own life.

It is the lack of urgency in regard to the present that makes us sin against the high moments which come to us. Instead of remembering them and living by them and acting on them, we allow their memories to fade from us without having done anything to ensure their commemoration. There is no individual who has not experienced far visions and times of deep insight. Often the difference between great living and cheap living is simply the failure to understand that those shining moments demand action now. We have not learned to live very wisely until we have learned it is possible to be too late. It is not always true that if we do not grasp the opportunity now, we will have a chance to grasp it later. The wrong vote cast, our failure to act here, or a wasted moment there may

[1] *Midnight on the Desert* (New York: Harper & Bros., 1937), p. 285.

affect life profoundly and lastingly. That diligent worker Charles Wesley complained in his diary that he fell from his horse and was sorely injured, "which prevented me writing hymns till next day."

Great men have always believed in the value of the passing moment. The genius with his profound vision and his grasp of eternal values has, at the same time, been very jealous of the use of time. There is a story of how Vincent d'Indy became the pupil of César Franck. The younger man had resented very much Franck's comments written on the score of one of his quartets. Sometime later, however, when he was looking back over that quartet and the criticisms, he was much impressed by noting that the changes suggested by the master were obviously improvements. He sought Franck out at once and asked if he could not become his pupil.

"Certainly," was the reply. "You may come to me every day at six o'clock."

"But, Master," was the answer, "that will surely interrupt your supper hour."

"Oh, no," answered Franck, smiling, "I mean six o'clock in the morning."

The word which comes to the Christian is, "Choose you this day." Indeed, he has the sense that every choice is a choice of life and death, and that so many implications hang in the balance that he must regard every passing moment as having eternal possibilities. If the Christian is unhurried, he is not unmindful of time. If he has learned not to fret himself because of the evildoer, he has also been warned that in such an hour as he thinks not the Son of Man comes. He must, therefore, be ready. No man knows what a day may bring forth, but the Christian knows that the present moment is to be used for the service of God.

The Eternal Now

The Christian comes to live in a great eternal now. Eternity breaks in upon his life here, and each moment partakes of the nature of the centuries. A British teacher some years ago bitingly analyzed the "politics" of a university faculty:

A *Conservative Liberal* is a broad-minded man, who thinks that something ought to be done. . . .

A *Liberal Conservative* is a broad-minded man, who thinks that something ought to be done. . . .

The men of both these parties are alike in being open to conviction; but so many convictions have already got inside, that it is very difficult to find the openings. They dwell in the Valley of Indecision.

The *Non-placet* differs in not being open to conviction; he is a man of principle. A principle is a rule of inaction. . . .

The *Adullamites* are dangerous, because they know what they want; and that is, all the money there is going. . . .

The *Young Man in a Hurry* is a narrow-minded and ridiculously youthful prig, who is inexperienced enough to imagine that something might be done before very long, and even to suggest definite things.[2]

The Christian, when he really understands the gospel's concept of the contemporary and the timeless, is a man who escapes all of the positions satirized above. To him there is always another dimension which keeps breaking in upon every moment and redeeming it from triviality. There is something about the experience of getting acquainted with Jesus Christ that gives a man a sense of having entered eternity here and now. Ezra Pound one time defined literature as news that stays news. So the gospel, old as it may be, is still the news that stays news and is contemporary in its significance and its meaning. It becomes a strange mixture of time and timelessness, for God gives to the Christian something of the sense that time is forever and eternity is now.

Thus it is that the Christian finds himself uncaptured by the past, yet having a deep respect and love for it. He finds himself unworried about tomorrow and not impatient when things do not move as fast as he desires. He understands at last that he is called upon to do his duty now. Although he has forever, the present moment is precious. Thus he is freed from slavery to time.

Rear Admiral Richard E. Byrd in describing his second trip to

[2] F. M. Cornford, *Microcosmographia Academica* (1922; reprint, University of Chicago Press, 1945).

the South Pole wrote: "All the time we continued flying as closely as possible along the 180th meridian. Even without wind drift, for which adequate corrections could be made, it is obvious that no navigator can fly along a mathematical line. Consequently, since this is the international date line, we were zigzagging constantly from today into tomorrow and back again." [3] That is precisely what happens to the Christian. He goes from yesterday into today into tomorrow and then back again. There is something about the experience of Jesus Christ that eliminates the barriers of time and puts a man into the midst of an eternal present. The Christian lives in the present as a creature of eternity, and he lives in eternity as if it had broken into this present moment and were a present experience.

[3] "Our Navy Explores Antarctica," National Geographic, Oct., 1947, p. 463.

XII

WEAKNESS AND STRENGTH

For when I am weak, then am I strong.—II Cor. 12:10

In the published diaries of Goebbels there are two or three references to Gandhi. In each case Goebbels refers to him as a fool and a fanatic. He intimates that if the Indian leader had had sense enough to organize militarily, he might have hoped to win the freedom of India. But Goebbels was sure Gandhi could never succeed by following the path of nonresistance and peaceful revolution. Now we see that India has obtained her independence, and Nazi Germany has been destroyed. It would appear that what this Nazi leader regarded as weakness was strength, and what he thought was strength was actually weakness.

In the days of Jesus his enemies looked at him much the same as Goebbels looked at Gandhi. Those in power did not take him very seriously. Rome had little to fear if these radicals were tended to promptly, and when he was crucified, the Roman officials were sure this man was finished. The path of sacrifice and suffering never seemed to the power worshipers of the first century to be the path of triumph and ultimate victory. They too mistook weakness for strength.

The same spirit is characteristic of our time. The Christian way is to us the impractical way, which is to say the weak way. We have not been convinced by the gospel's judgment that what we oftentimes look upon as strength is really weakness. We do not know what Paul meant when he wrote, "When I am weak, then am I strong." It is time, therefore, that we re-examine this strange paradox of the gospel. It assumes that only when men are aware of their weakness are they strong, and when men think they are powerful, that is the time they are in danger.

The Danger of Power

Let us look at this matter of power and consider its dangers. It is reported that when Stalin was asked by Laval not to antagonize the pope, he replied, "How many divisions does he have?" Here is an illustration of what power does to men. It makes them over-confident. It blinds their eyes to reality.

The Old Testament is full of stories which point up this truth. Samson is one of the best illustrations. Physically the most powerful man of his time, he could not believe that anyone was capable of overcoming him. He did not understand the power of Delilah. It is too bad he could not have read some of the modern advertisements which warn, "Never underestimate the power of a woman." Not until it was too late did Samson realize that his own feeling of power had betrayed him.

Or look at the story of Belshazzar. At the very height of the Babylonian king's might the hand comes writing along the wall, warning of his immediate destruction. In the midst of his feast of triumph and arrogance his fate is announced: "Your kingdom shall be given to the Medes and the Persians." The drama of the incident is in the fact that at the moment of his apparent success his doom had been decided. "In that night Belshazzar the Chaldean king was slain." (Dan. 5:30.)

In modern times we have an example. When the Second World War began, France had the largest and what was thought to be the most powerful conscript army in the world. Military experts said that Germany had moved too fast. She would break herself against the Maginot Line and would find herself overwhelmed by France's great army. But what happened? In about six weeks France was overrun because what she had thought would be her power was really her weakness. She had gone to sleep under a bureaucracy that had assumed routine training and mere numbers meant protection for the nation. Any coach with a winning team knows that the thing to dread most of all is the overconfidence which infects winning players. For when a team comes to think it is invincible, that is the time when some second- or third-rate team, with nothing to lose and everything to win, comes through to defeat the champion. The danger of power is the danger of overconfidence.

So it is with men facing temptations. Too many times instead of fleeing from spiritual danger they approach it with the idea that they can resist though all others fall. Many a man has gone down to moral disaster simply because he was too sure of his own power. Too many men ask for the tragedy which comes to them because they think that they are not as other men.

It is power that corrupts. It makes men lose their respect for human rights and human dignity. It brings pride into their hearts, which is to say they come to feel superior to the moral law and human rights. The lust for power works like termites, boring from within and leaving an outside shell that appears strong. But inside there has been a rottenness at work which weakens.

Max Eastman tells about visiting with a man in a sanitarium who threw out his chest as if he were about to receive a medal and said: "I have had insomnia for twenty years at a stretch, and there is just one thing will cure it. Many is the night I've got up at twelve or one and slipped around the corner for a swig of whisky. I don't take no drugs, but give me seven or eight whiskies and I'll sleep like a lamb. It's Christian Science, that's what I believe in—Christian Science and pure will power backed up by whisky!" [1] This is the effect of power upon men. They come to believe in pure will power and whisky, and at the end of the day it turns out that these are the things which have destroyed them. They are betrayed by a false sense of security.

WEAKNESS OF POWER

Not only does power have great dangers; it also has great weaknesses. The Christian believes that we do well to be aware of the

[1] *Enjoyment of Living* (New York: Harper & Bros., 1948), p. 243.

weakness of force. It overlooks the essentials about human life. The failure of all tyranny, since the beginning, has been that the time comes when it no longer can comprehend what human life is and what human life demands. When the tyrant has had his way for too long, he assumes that he can do anything he desires in his dealings with weaker men. He comes to the false conclusion that by making people afraid he can force them to follow any path he chooses. But men are made for freedom, and they will not go on forever without that essential. To ignore this truth is the weakness of tyranny.

Power is weak because it underestimates the unseen. It loses the ability to comprehend the meaning of faith and the might of the spirit. These are things which it dismisses easily, subscribing to the falsehood that only the big battalions count. It is true that only the strong can be free. Yet a strength without the support of faith and a sense of righteousness does not have lasting power. It thrives on victories, but it does not know how to endure defeats. When the going is difficult, there is no substitute for faith and the spiritual undergirding of a great tradition. The unswerving steadfastness of the democracies was a mystery to the Nazis. It is a mystery to any man or nation that has lost the knowledge that the greatest allies of men are the unseen forces of the spirit.

The weakness of power is that it cannot understand its own limitations. It does not comprehend that it can go only so far and no farther. It forgets that there is an impregnable fortress in the human heart. It does not remember that even the slave can choose death. Respect and devotion and loyalty, which are necessary for the strong foundation of any society, are not for sale and cannot be forced. They must be given freely, and the tyrant discovers that he has no way to obtain them. Yet they are necessities if he is to be safe. We might paraphrase and reverse a statement of Paul by saying that when men think they are strong, then they are weak, for there is terrible weakness in power.

Phillips Brooks told a story about an African missionary who came home on a furlough. Since he planned to return to his mission, he wanted to take his people a useful gift. He finally purchased a sundial, because he thought it would be helpful if the natives could tell the time. They liked the gift very much, but the first thing they did was to build a house around it to protect it. Power builds a house around the moral and spiritual sundial, and men no longer can tell the time. They do not know how late it really is. It insulates them from reality. Then while they are rejoicing in the false light of their success, the darkness comes and for them there is no dawn.

God's Use of Weakness

It is important to understand that God uses the methods of apparent weakness. Some men have looked at this fact and have totally misunderstood its implication, and so have misinterpreted it. Heine, for example, said that God had made a bargain with the devil, and had promised he would respect the devil's bailiwick and would expect the devil to do the same for him. Thus it was, Heine suggested, that both God and the devil are champions of the *status quo*. This misapprehension is due to the fact that God does not move along the road of force. He chooses the indirect way and the slow way. He oftentimes uses the method which seems to be ineffective.

The best example of that is Jesus Christ himself. That God should redeem the world through a peasant chosen from an obscure tribe at the east end of the Mediterranean Sea seems to most of us to be the most ridiculous of ideas. At least we would never have chosen that method. We would have chosen a man from the ruling race and the upper class. We would have taken him from Rome, not Nazareth. We would have sought a "key" person. God chose a Jew. Remember the lines:

> How odd of God
> To choose the Jews!

We look at the methods of God, and we are always saying, "How odd he was!" Then that he should choose for the Messiah this man who was to be crucified and killed seemed, above everything else, the most impossible way. It contradicts all our worldly cleverness.

At the very announcement of the coming birth of Jesus, the Gospel writer brings out, there was understanding that God was using the weak to confound the mighty. You remember Mary's song of joy as recorded in Luke:

> He hath showed strength with his arm;
> He hath scattered the proud in the imagination of their heart.
> He hath put down princes from their thrones,
> And hath exalted them of low degree.
> The hungry he hath filled with good things;
> And the rich he hath sent empty away.
> He hath given help to Israel his servant,
> That he might remember mercy
> (As he spake unto our fathers)
> Toward Abraham and his seed for ever. (1:51-55.)

This was the great word of faith spoken by men who had confidence that when God chose a baby to humble the mighty, the years would vindicate his choice. And so they have. Jesus remains today a barrier against which the power wielders break themselves. Kingdoms rise and fall, but his kingdom remains forever. Instead of seeking to be a despot, he puts forth every effort to keep himself from being made one.

Or we may look at the Church as an example of God's use of weakness. The early Christian fellowship was made up of the most humble of people. It did not begin at the top; it began at the bottom. No one looking at it would have thought it had any chance at all to exist, especially when the empire decided to stamp it out. Yet the Church has spread throughout the world until in 1948 there was held the first great World Council of Churches. It has penetrated into the life of Western civilization, affecting its standards and its sense of values. Strangely enough, the very times when it used the methods of power it was the weakest. The Church is always at its worst and least effective when it depends upon political connections and wealth. Its greatest strength has been when it understood Paul's word, "When I am weak, then am I strong."

Go back to the beginning of every great revolution and you discover, not a marching army, but a few men with ideas and a dream. The revolutions which have really affected life and meant progress have appeared as the most hopeless things at the beginning. Yet there is something irresistible about a small group of men with an idea whose time has come.

In the physical universe we have the example of the atom. The tremendous power which we fear in our world is not the flow of great rivers or the floods which they cause. It is not the might of the tide as it pushes the millions of tons of water forward and then draws them back again. It is not the flash of the lightning or the crack of the thunder. It is something so small that we cannot see it. It is the atom which we fear, for it is the atom which has the unlimited power to blow the world apart. What would seem to be the weakest thing in the world is in reality an unbelievably powerful force. So it is that God in his dealing with humanity uses, not the great spectacular things which rulers use, but the insignificant things which men despise.

How true this has been in the history of Christianity! Here is Paul against the Roman Empire—one man against the established paganism. Enemies within and enemies without, yet this one man, with all his weakness, which he knew so well, established the Christian Church throughout the world and is forever the symbol of its ultimate triumph. Our strength has been, not in the Constantines but in the saints and martyrs. So often the saint was a martyr. The world could take his life and use his death as a means of entertainment. Young and old, men and women marched in that gallant procession of sacrifice. But the saints and martyrs built a foundation upon which the future of Christian culture rested. By their weakness we are made strong.

One of the groups most deeply affecting society has been the Quakers. They have not believed in force and have been a humble people. Yet, when it comes to the reconstruction work of the world, they are the ones who have contributed so much beyond what we might expect from their actual number. There is a wonderful story about a Quaker. He heard a strange noise in his house at night and slipped downstairs to see what it was. There he found a burglar busily at work. Pointing his gun at him, the Quaker said gently, "Friend, I would do thee no harm for the world and all that is in it, but thou standest where I am about to shoot." The burglar was soon gone.

So it has been time after time in human experience. The weak groups who say gently, "You are standing in the place where we intend to go," have within them irresistible power which nothing can stop. How many times they have spoken their warning against hatred and prejudice and injustice. How characteristic they are of the way God moves. If we had ears to hear, we would hear him saying to every power-mad man, "My son, you are obstructing the way I intend to go. You will either change your life, or you will be destroyed."

Power of Weakness

We come at last to see the truth of Paul's insight that there is tremendous power in what the world calls weakness. This is one of the things about the Christian gospel which men find very difficult to comprehend. To admit weakness, in the world's viewpoint, is the worst possible thing a man can do. But from the standpoint of the Christian faith it is the first necessary thing to do. It is as if God's strength cannot be ours so long as we lack a sense of our need for it. Paul speaks out of his own experience. As long as he labored under the delusion that he could work out his own salvation, he went from failure to despair. The vision on the Damascus Road dissolved his confidence in his own strength. That was the beginning of his salvation.

It has been popular in our time to assume that the dictator's power was his appeal to the worst in human nature. He called forth selfishness, hatred, bigotry, and prejudice. The fear was expressed that if a democratic government appealed to the best in men, it would be no match for such a system. All of this is quite false. Nothing is quite so powerful as the hunger for goodness in the human heart. Men can never escape it, and it moves like a mighty tide, irresistible, overwhelming everything in its path.

Each man knows, in his own quiet moment, that what he wants above everything else is goodness and decency in his life. The more he seeks to deny this knowledge, and the more he seeks to lose himself in lust and selfishness, the more irresistible becomes this hunger for goodness. It breaks through into his consciousness whenever he is off guard. The appeal to the worst in men has a temporary victory, but it is a cheap one, and it does not endure. It is the appeal to goodness, with all its apparent weakness, that represents the strength of a movement and the might of a people.

We cannot understand how much power there is in sacrifice. In much of our thinking sacrifice represents defeat, for the man who is successful does not have to give up; he can demand what he wants and take it. Cutting straight across this philosophy we have the Cross. Nothing that ever happened to the human race has had its power. Nothing has been such a rallying center for the best in human life as that symbol of crucifixion. It teaches us to attain what we really want by surrendering what we know in our best moments is unworthy of us.

We have been through a bitter period when we were told by many so-called realists that we must hate in order to win. We were told that all this Christian talk about love is all right in its place, but not when we are face to face with a dangerous enemy. Yet the hatred which seems to be irresistible soon breaks itself against the overpowering might of love. For all hate can do is destroy. It never builds, and the need of men is for reconstruction. After hate has done its worst, then the simple power of love moves in and completes what hate failed to accomplish. Jesus did not choose the way of love because it was a nice way. He chose it because he believed that it was the best way, the most powerful way. Let us once again paraphrase the apostle's word: "When I hate, I am weak; but when I love, then am I strong."

It is in the light of this that we must understand the Beatitudes of Jesus. He is talking about a reality that is not apparent to our eyes. It is the humble, the poor, the pure in heart who find the deepest joys in life and possess the future. Yet the Beatitudes represent nonsense to a great number of people and utter weakness to most of us. We cannot believe that the kind of man Jesus talks about in these strange teachings of his has an endurance that the worldly powerful cannot know.

Here we find the meaning of the parable of the publican and the Pharisee. The Pharisee represents the person who is aware of his own moral superiority. He speaks for many of us when he says, "I thank God that I am not as other men." Most of us, as we look around, are grateful that we do not live in the slums or on the level of the degraded. It is too easy for us to lift our eyes to heaven and be grateful for our obvious superiority. How many of us can find the grace to take our place with the publican? Not many of us are sensitive enough to our own needs and our own failures to keep our heads bowed and pray to be forgiven for our pride. Yet the judgment of Jesus falls hardest upon the Pharisee and most gently upon the publican. Once again we see at work this paradox, "When I am weak, then am I strong."

Rossini was asked one time to write an opera for a certain company whose contralto had only one good note, a middle B-flat. No one would have blamed Rossini if he had said that no one in his right mind could expect a man to write a successful opera so handicapped. But without uttering a word of complaint he wrote his opera. He created for the contralto a recitative on middle B-flat and had the orchestra and the chorus weave a glorious harmony all around it. It was one of his greatest arias. That is the way God does with us. Many of us have hardly one good note. But if we are aware of our lack, he will use what little we have and make something triumphant and beautiful. To cover up our weakness is failure. To pretend to a power we do not have is tragedy. But to face our weakness and hand it over to God is to find a strength we did not know was there. Once again the gospel leads us into a reversal of our worldly wisdom. What we think is power is weakness, but what we know is our weakness can become our strength. "When I am weak," says Paul, "then am I strong."

XIII

NARROW AND WIDE

Enter ye in by the narrow gate.   —Matt. 7:13
Thou hast set me at large when I was in distress.   —Ps. 4:1

IT IS REPORTED THAT A SCOTCH MINISTER IN CANADA ONCE OFFERED
the following prayer:

O Lord, we approach Thee this morning in an attitude of prayer and
likewise of complaint. When we came to Canada we expected to find
a land flowing with milk and honey, but instead we find a land peopled
with the ungodly Irish. O Lord, in Thy mercy drive them to the utter-
most parts of Canada, make them hewers of wood and drawers of water,
give them no places as magistrates, policemen, or rulers among Thy
people. But if Ye have any favors to bestow or any good land to give
away, give it to Thine own peculiar people, the Scots. Make them members of Parliament, rulers among Thy people, but as for the ungodly
Irish, take them by the heels and shake them over the mouth of hell,
but Lord, don't let them fall in, and the glory shall be Thine forever.
Amen.

In a rebellion against the narrowness and bigotry reflected in a
prayer of this kind our age has gone to an extreme in the other
direction and become tolerant of everything and everyone. We
awaken to the unpleasant truth that a great deal of what we call
tolerance is really indifference. Men are tempted to become narrow
and bigoted when they are dealing with something which concerns
them profoundly and which they consider to be of the utmost importance. Tolerance is a very easy virtue when we do not care one

way or the other. In the name of being broad and unbiased we have tended to become shallow and unconcerned.

One of the fundamental problems of human life is to hold great convictions and at the same time be tolerant. How does a man hold to essential beliefs without bigotry? How does he escape the dry rot of indifference? How can he realize the truth of Jesus' assertion that life is to be found by entering a narrow gate, and also respond to the pressure our religion puts upon us to expand our vision and broaden our sympathies? This is another one of those paradoxes of Christianity which are a sign of its depth and realism.

The Evil of Bigotry

There can be no doubt that there is an evil bigotry which is the enemy of Christ. Frederick Faber's hymn expresses this truth very clearly:

> For the love of God is broader
>   Than the measure of man's mind,
> And the heart of the Eternal
>   Is most wonderfully kind.
>
> But we make his love too narrow
>   By false limits of our own;
> And we magnify his strictness
>   With a zeal he will not own.

The literalist is the man who makes the gospel unnecessarily repulsive by his failure to comprehend its spirit. When any man begins to put too much emphasis upon words and sentences instead of on the truth he is trying to express through them, the result can never be a very happy one. Many an individual has been turned away from the Christian gospel by a feeling that if this narrow interpretation was legitimate, it could not be for him. It seemed to be an utter denial of the spirit of God, as well as the spirit of his Son.

A legalistic theology has the same effect upon men's minds. We ought never to assume that we can reduce the way God deals

140

with men to mechanical rules. The confidence some Christians have in defining the limitations of the way God works with men reveals that their idea of God is a very small one and a very limited one. Back of much conservative teaching about the Atonement has been the assumption that God was no greater than the most narrow-minded judge, or else he was caught in his own legalities. It is no wonder that a number of sincere people have felt that such mechanical theology was not for them, and they must find their way to God by some other path.

It would be well for all the little interpreters of God to read over and over again George MacDonald's famous lines:

> Here lie I, Martin Elginbrodde;
> Hae mercy o' my soul, Lord God,
> As I wad do, were I Lord God,
> An ye were Martin Elginbrodde.

The bigotry which assumes a finality of thought is always a dangerous thing in any realm. Whenever men come to believe that every truth has been ultimately stated and needs no reinterpretation and re-examination, they begin to put more emphasis upon authority than upon light. They tend to regard facts as a drunkard regards a lamppost—something to lean against instead of something to illuminate the darkness. This spirit has done our faith much harm. It has been a denial of the wideness of God's mercy, and it has failed to comprehend the continual presence of the Holy Spirit in our lives and thoughts.

That same narrow intolerance has been too characteristic of our social thinking in days past. We have been too much the victim of those who assume that race relations have been settled finally and ultimately and that each race ought to have its place and keep it. It is the assumption that once a color has been established in a man's skin, he has been forever cabined and confined. There has been as much ridiculous nonsense taught about the theory of the limitation of what men can do because of their color as about any other social phenomenon in our human experience.

141

A narrow patriotism can become the most dangerous thing in the world. A patriotism which assumes that a nation is to be regarded as if it were the whole world finally so blinds the citizens of that nation with pride that the country is easily destroyed. The real argument against a narrow nationalism is not merely that it is bad—though it is. Rather it is that an extreme nationalistic outlook invites disaster. When a people think more highly of themselves than they ought to think, they become an embarrassment to God's larger aims. In their blindness they stand in the way of processes which finally crush them. The bigoted point of view ignores certain essentials which if neglected mean death. It is the same with class. A class-conscious man is only half alive and only half alert to the reality of the human situation. When the narrow bigot has his way in interpreting race or nation or class, doom lies in wait for him.

It should be recognized that bigotry is not necessarily confined to conservative people. There is such a thing as a liberal intolerance. Let no man assume that because he has outgrown the inadequate theology of a past century, he has entered automatically into the liberal spirit. We have been as much victimized by the intolerances of modernism as we have by the reactionary spirit of an embalmed orthodoxy. One of the sad sights of our day is the self-confessed liberal who has made his materialistic science as closed a system as his grandfather's fundamentalism ever was. The difficulties of our time are not due to the liberal spirit, but to the fact that we have not had it. We have traded one bigotry for another and merely changed its label.

A Harvard anthropologist, Professor Clyde Kluckhohn, made this biting remark concerning people who find their superiority in their ancestors:

By the laws of chance essentially every person whose ancestry is at least half European is descended from Charlemagne. But he is equally descended from the bandit hanged on the hill, from the half-witted serf, and from every other person living in 800 A.D. who left as many descendants as did Charlemagne. The principal difference between the snob and "lower-class" citizen is that the former has the money to pay a genealogist to trace or to fake plausibly a lineage.[1]

And this narrow-minded exclusiveness, whether it be applied to genealogy or to science or to society, is something against which every man ought to fight. That is especially true if he finds a tendency toward it in his own life, as most of us do.

THE NARROW GATE

Yet on the other hand there is a narrow gate through which we must enter if we are to find life. There are some things which are not to be compromised and never to be surrendered. We learn sooner or later that until a man has some things he will defend unto death, he has nothing for which he can really live. We cannot have everything in life. To have the important things demands the ability to discriminate. The man who will not make up his mind but dabbles in every interesting possibility is the man whose very wideness makes him shallow. If it is necessary to be broad enough to escape narrowness, it is also necessary to be narrow enough to be deep.

Religion has taught men always that there are sacred things which are above price. They are to a man's life what the holy of holies was to the Jewish temple. That was the central place where God dwelt and where no man could enter except the priest. That was the place never to be invaded, and a man must give up his life in its defense. It is so easy to compromise sacred values until, literally, it is true that a price has been set on everything. It is very easy to believe that each man has his price if one knows in his heart that he has his own. He learns to laugh at the strange ideas his brethren have of things which are not to be done. But the years proclaim that the man who has lost all sense of sacred things is also the man whose life has become merely a noisy gong and a clanging cymbal. And if to the world without it seems that these sacred things represent

[1] *Religion and Our Racial Tensions*, Vol. III of "Religion in the Post-War World" series, ed. W. L. Sperry (Cambridge: Harvard University Press, 1945), pp. 14-15.

narrowness, intolerance, and bigotry, then so be it. We know also that they represent loyalties without which life becomes cheap and trivial.

The Christian is so concerned with the worth of every man's life that he is oftentimes accused of being very narrow and intolerant. He makes a great objection, for example, to gambling, and the man of the world asks himself what is so serious about this apparently harmless pastime. The Christian, however, is aware that the gambling habit, once established, will destroy a man's integrity and his honor. He is quite willing to be thought of as narrow if he can use his influence against something which sooner or later cheapens the worth of men. The amusements of life which appeal to so many individuals and do no immediately apparent harm are often looked upon suspiciously by the Christian. He would be hard put to tell why a particular amusement is bad in itself, but he knows that if indulged in over a period of years it cheapens men in their own eyes. It is habit forming, and time spent on it is time wasted. Against anything of that kind he sets his face as a rock. He is the most intolerant man in the world when it comes to condoning practices which do not make men better.

So far as his own integrity is concerned, the Christian appears to be very intolerant. From the days when Christians refused to pay even lip service to the deity of the Roman emperor until the day Christians refused to bow down before Hitler they have realized that at all costs they must maintain their personal freedom in God. The Christian would much rather be regarded as a bigot by his brethren, but at the same time be able to live with himself in peace, than to have the praise of men and despise himself. He has learned that to achieve self-respect he must be willing to enter the narrow gate and suffer the criticism and sarcasm of the masses who go carelessly through the wide gate to the broad path.

A man and his wife and two children had been visiting the museum at the University of Nebraska. They were obviously in town on a tour. The children asked to go upstairs. The parents were not too anxious, and were overheard conferring about it.

"Do you know what's upstairs?" the father asked the mother.

"The art gallery," she replied.

"You see, children!" the father said, "you don't need to go up there; there's nothing up there but art."

How characteristic that is of us! We ask, "What will we find through that narrow gate?" Someone may reply that we will find a sense of the sacred and an understanding of the worth of a man's life. "Oh," we inquire, "if that's all there is, why go through the narrow gate to find that?" But at last we discover that those were the things which could have made our life significant. By missing them we missed everything.

The Wideness of the Gospel

Yet, lest we assume that the gospel is to be symbolized only by a narrow gate, we had better understand also that it is as wide as the universe. Its interests can never be confined to any small area of human life. Whatever is of human significance is of significance to the gospel. As a matter of fact, no one lives in quite so wide a world as does the Christian. There is no person whose horizons are pushed farther back than his.

This is something which a good many people can never quite understand about Christianity. They want to confine it to certain places and to certain situations. They say, for example, that it never ought to have anything to do with politics. How often a preacher who has the prophet's conviction that God's word is for the political leaders is criticized for entering a field which should not be of his concern. We in America have inherited a belief in the separation of church and state. We are proud of it, and there is no desire on the part of Protestant leaders, any more than of political leaders, to break down this separation. Christians who understand the American genius are especially suspicious of any religious group which moves in the direction of political power and religious monopoly. We do not want a state church. Yet we are quite wrong if we assume that the Church has nothing to say about politics.

The Church stands as the conscience of society, and as long as men are political creatures and have political relationships, the Church will be concerned about them. It will demand the freedom to discuss and to criticize national programs. A religion unconcerned about the foreign policy of a nation or about its international commitments and relationships would be an emasculated faith with nothing about it to challenge the loyalty of realistic men. That the Church should become a political institution is unthinkable. But Christians should understand that their faith is no less authoritative when they are acting politically than when they are in the act of worship.

The whole meaning of the social gospel has been an insistence on the relevance of Christianity to every condition of man. In more modern times it has been the gospel's attempt to minister in an industrial society. But the idea of a social gospel did not begin in the twentieth century. It is certainly as old as Amos, and it has never been lacking in any age since God spoke to Moses. When men intimate that their religion can become confined to a particular institution, to a particular day of the week, or to a particular situation, they simply confess their utter misunderstanding of the meaning of Christianity.

As a matter of fact this gospel of ours is the most persistent thing in the world, and the most demanding. Its holiness is not just a matter of respecting the taboos of a deity. Christian holiness has ethical meaning and social implications. If the so-called "holiness groups" are trying to impress our generation with this truth, very good. But if they are endeavoring to make the gospel the inspiration for a narrow emotional experience, then they have missed the way. Holiness, like all the Christian virtues, is known by its fruits. Pretend as we will, it is no longer possible for any Western Christian to be at peace with himself when he knows there is a realm in his life which defies the authority of Christ. For the gospel understands that one unredeemed part of a man can destroy all the rest. In that it is a little like price control. We cannot control the price of one product and expect our economy to be balanced. Nor can one part of our life be redeemed while the other is left under the law of the jungle.

That is to say, of course, that the gospel is a way of life and not an intellectual exercise. It knows nothing about boundaries and limitations. It is not aware of any place where a man can enter and leave his faith behind him. It will have nothing to do with the idea that certain activities are to be justified on the basis of expediency. Whatever concerns human life concerns the gospel, and wherever there are forces which affect human life the gospel will demand its right to challenge and affect those forces.

The gospel's ultimate concern is with people. When Kagawa was visiting in Boston, he was asked what buildings he would like to see. He replied, "I'm not interested in architecture; take me where they are doing things to help people!" This is the word of the Christian. Architecture, historical points of interest are all right, but the ultimate things about a city are the activities which are going on to help people. What effect does this thing have upon children or upon homes? is the Christian's question. The gospel always demands its right to ask such questions and to judge any policy in the light of the answer. If there is the narrow gate in the Christian gospel, there is also in it the breadth of all humanity and the wideness of the universe.

Salvation by Expansion

One of the things hardest to understand about Christianity is its offer of salvation by way of expansion. A man's sickness is often-times due to his exclusiveness, and his healing is possible only when he breaks that down. Trees in a Brazilian forest, for example, depend upon each other. A single tree can hardly stand up against the variation of temperature, the floods, the winds. The trees need to associate in a forest. There is no doubt that every tree must lose something of its individuality in the process, but it gains the strength by which it can survive. And men are like that. More times than not the answer is to bring the lonely man into fellowship with his brethren.

There is no better example of this principle than grief. How do we cure a broken heart? How do we overcome the devastation of sorrow? Our instinct says to withdraw and nurse that sorrow and make it the center of all our thoughts. We are tempted to live with it day and night, as if it were to be our constant companion forever. Strangely enough, oftentimes our healing begins only when we try to help someone else. To alleviate our distress the gospel urges us to expand. The fourth psalm states this principle by saying that God answered the psalmist's call for help by enlarging him when he was in distress. This man had learned he had been living in too narrow a place. His trouble had closed in upon him, and his salvation was in breaking through it to the world of God's peace.

We discover how to cure our anxiety by action. The stubborn refusal to participate in the group encourages the growth of worry and unhappiness. Once we have decided on an activity that is before us and have resolved to begin it, we are on the way to overcoming our fear and grief. And there is always something we can do. There is, as a matter of fact, always something we ought to do and are called by our conscience to do. In a great number of instances victorious living begins the moment we decide to do the one good, unselfish thing which stands waiting in plain sight.

Only love can overcome hatred, and love demands relationships. It demands that we pray for the one we hate. It demands that we stop nursing that bitterness and gain our release from it through service. The gospel comes to men who are enmeshed in these destroying emotions and speaks the same word which God spoke to Abraham, "Get thee out of thy country, and from thy kindred, and from thy father's house, unto the land that I will show thee." (Gen. 12:1.) We are saved by expansion.

In a conversation with Cardinal Manning, Henry George said, "I love the people, and that love brought me to Christ as their best friend and teacher."

Manning replied, "And I loved Christ and so learned to love the people for whom he died." So, no matter where you begin, you will be led ultimately to the people and to the wideness of the world. Thus in some mysterious way the paradox is resolved. You enter by way of the narrow gate, but you come ultimately into the vast expanses of God's eternal and all-inclusive kingdom.

XIV

DESPAIR AND HOPE

I know how to be abased, and I know also how to abound.
—Phil. 4:12

THERE ARE TWO CLASSES OF PEOPLE IN THE WORLD WHO DO MUCH
harm. They are the professional optimists and the professional
pessimists. They make being optimistic or pessimistic a career.
The professional optimist is the one who is always sure that
everything will be all right. Jeremiah refers to him as one who
cries "Peace, peace," when there is no peace. He is the man who
does not see reality but always blurs the unpleasant with pretense.
He believes that wishing will make it so. He believes that if we
pretend everything is well, things will actually turn out that way.
You see him sometimes in business groups, insisting that the way
to make business good is to pretend that it is good. When you are
feeling sad and distressed, he is the fellow who slaps you on the
back and says, "Cheer up, old man. Around the corner there is a
bluebird." So far as I am concerned, nothing could make me feel
worse. He is a dangerous person because he hinders men from doing
the things necessary for salvation. President Eliot said about Harvard: "Things seem to be going fairly well now that a spirit of
pessimism prevails in all departments."

The other man is the professional pessimist. For him nothing is
ever right and nothing is ever hopeful. Whenever there is one
promising possibility, he can see a hundred things which may prevent it. He helps to create the very thing he fears. His mood of
hopelessness encourages evil. It is difficult to tell which of these

150

two types is the worst. A false optimism leads to destruction, and so does a false pessimism. Both viewpoints are shallow and unrealistic.

Paul describes the Christian experience as an ability to face the evil and believe in the good. His word to us is, "I know how to be abased, and I know also how to abound." He writes those words from prison as he faces a very uncertain future. He is saying to his beloved friends at Philippi that he has been through the best and the worst, the optimistic and the pessimistic, and he has discovered something that helps him to deal with both of those conditions. The despair that drives many men to ruin only makes the Christian more firm. The hope which makes many a man lose his head only makes the Christian calm. Nowhere is the sign of the greatness of our faith more apparent than in its ability to help men go through despair and hope and be content in either situation.

Despair in the Human Situation

We must begin by confessing that human life has within it the element of despair. No man looks at his own soul with any honesty without feeling a hopelessness beyond his power to overcome. This despair is caused by a gap between what man is and what he knows he ought to be. We cannot escape the feeling that we were made for greatness, and we cannot escape the conviction that we fall far beneath that state. Paul gave this experience its classic expression in the seventh chapter of Romans, when he talked about doing the evil he did not really want to do. The human situation has at the very heart of it an element of tragedy. We are all disappointed men.

This is a part of the mystery of humanity. This is the thing which differentiates it from all animal life. So far as we can tell, no animal has this sense of despair so deeply embedded in its very nature. Even when the world looks upon us as successful, that failure is apparent to our own eyes. It is not a despair caused by a failure to attain things. It is a despair caused by our failure to be what we know God and our hearts demand us to be. Any philosophy of life that does not begin with the reality of this despair in humanity is

151

inadequate. It cannot last very long, and it cannot minister to our needs. Whether we like it or not, each man has to begin with a hopelessness in his heart.

There is no intellectual way out, and the saddest failure of reason is its inability to find one. The philosopher can tell us what we ought to do, and we can agree with him. The philosopher can tell us what the laws of virtue are, and we can understand that. But the philosopher cannot tell us how to find power to do what we know we ought to do and what in our best moments we want to do. For our trouble is not lack of knowledge but lack of power. A generation which substitutes philosophy for religion gets along very well as long as things go smoothly. But in the hour of its disaster it knows that it has built upon the sand.

Education alone, as we know it in the United States, cannot help us out of this human dilemma. We Americans are worshipers of education, and we have believed that all problems could be solved by following its path. We have assumed that if the time should come when each man is educated, then we would have solved the main problems of our society. Well, we have had universal education in the United States long enough now to draw some conclusions. We have succeeded to a marvelous extent in teaching our people to read and write. Have we become a happier people because of that? Is our political life on a higher plane because of the spread of literacy? Is our social life more virtuous because of academic progress? Mere facts do not make men better, and free public education by itself cannot bring in the Kingdom of God.

Can we solve this problem by the way of materialism? It has been our hope that in making life healthier we could remove the despair from the human heart. According to the standards which our fathers knew we have succeeded in this aim. Never has there been a generation with a better physical environment than this one. Never has the common man possessed more wealth than he possesses now. Never has the ordinary person had at his command more material power. Yet, instead of solving this human mystery, it has in some ways made it only more apparent. We are successes in every realm except in the realm that really matters. It should be apparent to all men by this time that the healing of the despair in human life by the intellectual method is a vain hope.

During the last war, when our GIs were scattered across the world, most of them were generous and friendly and made good impressions upon their hosts. Only now and again there comes to us a story like the one about a GI who was leaning precariously over the rail of a river boat in Bengal. A near-by Indian, in a friendly way, bade him take care since the river was full of hungry crocodiles. But the boy, turning and seeing a man with a dark skin, snarled back, "Mind your own business, nigger! I'll look out for myself!" He was speaking to a former premier of Bengal. All the good which a hundred men may have done for our racial relationships was undone by that one evil remark. This is the cause for despair in the human heart. This is where we go wrong. There is something in us which is evil and cruel and bigoted. How to destroy that evil thing is the question, and our failure to destroy it means despair.

Despair and Society

Society, like the individual, has within it the seeds of despair. Arnold Toynbee points out that there have been some twenty-one civilizations which have grown great and then have died. Some of them were almost as splendid as ours, and yet each one of them failed to solve its problems and went down. Historians have pointed out that the seeds of destruction in those other civilizations are observable within ours. It seems obvious that instead of learning very much from the past we follow a similar way, which brought them to death.

America in the nineteenth century knew a great social hopefulness. Americans believed they could solve the problems of society. Several experiments were conducted by groups of people who endeavored to form the perfect society in miniature. They would show that through co-operation and sharing it was possible to solve these fundamental evils of social life. Without any exception they failed. Sometimes they failed because of poor leadership. Sometimes they failed for lack of economic judgment. Sometimes they failed because of selfishness and bitterness among their members. But no Utopian society has thus far been established permanently and expanded.

Whenever men come together, there is set loose a cruel, inhuman competition. We in America remember when it was "big business" which we feared above everything else. The story of the robber barons is one of the disgraceful episodes in American life, for it tells of an antisocial exploitation of our natural resources and men. We remember the time when an industrial ruler said, "The public be damned." We remember how great corporations had the power and used the power to throttle competition and drive men to suicide.

Then labor came into its own. Labor became powerful, as it ought to be. It formed into great unions and became aware of its ability to challenge big business. Now over and against big business there stands big labor. We are aware that half a dozen men can keep the industrial wheels of America from turning. We are aware that one or two ruthless leaders now have it within their power to bring ruin to masses of men. Big labor often uses the same methods big business used. Labor is as great a danger potentially as business was a generation ago.

In order to arbitrate between big business and big labor it is necessary to create big government. The government comes further and further into our private lives because it is necessary. It must have more power to define what we can do and cannot do. But whenever we have big government, then we have the danger of a big bureaucracy that may fall into the hands of the demagogues. What was meant to be an arbitrator can become an exploiter and a betrayer. How to keep the power groups in society in check is a problem we have not yet solved.

In the world today we have great nations standing over against each other. Here is one world, and yet powerful empires act as if they were the only factors to be considered. The creation of giant empires and the reduction of smaller nations into relative insignificance has not helped us in establishing peace. Apparently we now have a new problem and in some ways a more serious one.

Reinhold Niebuhr's book with the significant title *Moral Man and Immoral Society* developed the thesis that while a man individually is usually decent, he often loses his moral sense when lost in a mass. Men become worse in crowds, for they seem to lose their sense of accountability. They will vote millions for war and pennies for housing. They will make all kinds of sacrifices to kill but no sacrifice at all to live. They will hurl their energies into destruction, but they will not lift their little fingers to help build.

How can we deal with this evil in human society? The old idea was called *laissez faire*, which meant to let everybody do as he pleases. This fine theory suggested that while somebody might get hurt in the process, finally it would all balance out, so it was best just to let the process go on. But no one can believe that today, for we know it cannot work. Society is so complicated it demands controls of some kind.

Somebody says socialism is the answer. It may be that public ownership of certain industries has much in its favor. Yet as we look at public control, we do not see any inevitable improvement. We know that merely to change masters is not necessarily to progress. A socialistic system, or any system, without individual character to hold it up could not work at all. If men have the necessary character, then private ownership will work too.

We remember how a few years ago the answer seemed to be totalitarianism. This was the promise that Hitler and his kind brought to the world. There were certain sacrifices to be made, to be sure, but they promised security. It would be hard for any American to believe those promises after what he has witnessed the past few years. Totalitarianism, which was supposed to free men from inequality, became a slavery which affected not only the poor but the rich. Nor do we change its essential evil when we call it Communism.

Can it be done by laws? Not completely. Laws, after all, have to have the public behind them, and if they do not have public support, they can be nullified. The law is always limited by the loyalty

155

and the devotion of the citizen. No matter what system we suggest, we are driven back finally to this fundamental truth: we cannot deal with the evil in society until the individual man is a better man. We have found no mechanical way of making him better, and we cannot find a fool-proof system to make society better. In this day when the world is so small our problem is so great. One good nation in the world is not enough. We are dependent upon each other, and one evil nation is a great threat to all mankind.

A student one time asked a professor, "Would it be possible for all the people of the world to live in the state of Texas?" The professor thought for a little while, estimated the size of the state and the number of people in the world, and answered: "Yes. It would be possible if they were all friends." There we have it. The evil in society goes back to the evil in the human heart. The seed of despair in society is the despair in the human situation. There is no answer until something can be done about that.

There Is Hope

But over on the other side of the picture there is something we can overlook. It is the fact that out of this despair there springs hope, which cannot be killed, no matter what is done to it. If despair is the last word, why cannot men simply accept the idea that they must live as beasts in the jungle? From whence come all the dreams of a better life for the individual and for society? The answer, I think, leads straight to God. It is because we are made in his image that we know there is an answer to human tragedy.

Some time ago a German historian and philosopher suggested that a society is like a human organism. It goes through its childhood, its youth, its adolescence, its maturity, and finally reaches its senility and dies. He intimated that because a civilization is like this, nothing could be done about it. He believed that we in the West were going down the other side of the hill, and all we could do was adjust ourselves to the melancholy fact that we were old and death was inevitable. But when Toynbee wrote *A Study of History*, he admitted that other civilizations had died and pointed out that

156

we show many of the signs of decay. But he would not admit that it is inevitable that we should follow that path. On the contrary, he went out of his way to say that it is not too late for us to be saved. You see, Arnold Toynbee is a Christian, and over against the despair, which he sees as clearly as anyone else, hope comes to his vision.

There is a sense in which Christian hope is impossible until one has faced the despair in the human situation. Two men were riding on a train, and as they passed through the slum section of a city, one man leaned over and pulled the curtain down, saying, "Since I can't do anything about that mess, at least I do not have to look at it." But the other man put the curtain up and said to his companion, "You can do something. You can look!" Christian hope does not begin with a refusal to look at the worst. It begins with the worst. For any victory which may come to us in life has to come to us out of conflict. The novelist always goes wrong when his plot suggests it is easy for things to turn out right and for everyone to live happily ever after. Life simply is not like that. Until a man has looked at the abyss which looms in front of every human soul, he can never know Christian hope. Until a man is aware of the darkness without God, he cannot really have his eyes open to see God. Oftentimes we go wrong when we assume that God can bring us his hopefulness without first of all letting us see what life would be without him.

Let us imagine that Jesus Christ did not die on the cross. Let us imagine that he fled for his safety when the opposition closed in upon him at Jerusalem, and he died many years later in bed. Let us assume he became a gentle old man, teaching nice things and writing books. Do you think that by any chance he could have become the Saviour of the world, or the Saviour of your life? Is it not true that Jesus Christ is the Saviour of men because he has experienced the worst? It is the Cross which is able to redeem mankind. We cannot believe that in some automatic way all of this was determined for him, but we are driven to the conclusion that it was his willingness to face the worst and endure the worst that made him our Redeemer. Christianity presents the strange paradox of a hope that springs out of a crucifixion, and a cross as a symbol of victory.

The hope of Christians is in their faith that they have a great destiny. For the Greeks the Golden Age was in the past, but for the Jew and the Christian the Kingdom of God is in the present and the future. It is the certainty that God has a plan and there is a

> far-off divine event,
> To which the whole creation moves,

which gives the Christian his assurance. He has the confidence that God's will must be done and that God's victory must be attained. To the extent that he yields his life to that eternal destiny he knows he has the firm basis of a great hope. He can say with Paul that present sufferings are not to be considered too seriously when one thinks of the glorious future which lies ahead.

The sensitive man has the feeling that something important has been left out of all the philosophies which end with despair. Somehow they do not go far enough, and they do not take into consideration all the depths of human experience. G. K. Chesterton went so far as to say that the men who finally brought him to orthodoxy were the atheists. As he put it, "They sowed in my mind my first wild doubts of doubt." The cynics have only half of the argument. They go only half the distance. For man is made to pass through the valley of doubt and despair and climb to the hills of hope and assurance.

One of my friends told me that the idea for the best sermon he ever preached came to him while listening to an atheist trying to disprove God. The one-sided philosophies of despair inspire the human mind to push on to hope. One of the most contradictory things in the world is the atheist's creation of faith, when it is the very thing he tries to destroy.

A strange affair that came out of the war was known as "The Hardy Case." Hardy was a member of the French Underground, and toward the end of the war it was suspected that he was the man who had been betraying his comrades to the Gestapo. When the war was over, he was brought to trial. But he had an able lawyer who managed to create so much doubt in the minds of the jury that his client was acquitted. Then after this was all over, Hardy admitted he was guilty. When asked why he had confessed after he had been declared innocent, he answered, "I couldn't live a lie forever." So it is that just when men are willing to say that humanity is bad, something like that happens, and they have to say that there is also an inescapable rectitude in it. Out of the despair of the human situation the Christian finds springing up a great hope.

Hope Is in God

The Christian learns that the basis of all hope is in God. This is extremely important. For the misplaced hopes of men lead to the worst disillusionment of all. We are being told continually that one swallow does not make a summer. And yet on an April afternoon when we see the first skimming bird our hearts leap up and tell us that the winter is over and the spring is here. Summer will not be far behind. So God comes to our hearts with the first intimations of a better life and a better future. Let us never get so old or so hopeless that we cannot respond to that promise of his. Let us know that our longings and our dreams are his gifts to us. It is this touch of God which makes it possible for us to act here and now. The despairing man has no power and does nothing. The optimist simply hopes for the best and does nothing. But the Christian feels his whole life lifted up to act.

What happens to men when they are disappointed? The fool blames the particular situation and comes to the conclusion that if he had a few more trinkets he would be happy. He decides that twenty thousand dollars did not do the job, so he needs a hundred thousand. He goes on his blundering way, hoping to find his answer in a greater abundance of things.

There is the disillusioned man who assumes finally that life is like that and he had better make up his mind not to hope for too much. He becomes bitter and cynical, and he insists that no one ought to expect very much out of life. This way is better than the first way, but not much better.

Then there is the Christian way which knows that the earth can never quite satisfy us, no matter how beautiful it is or how lovely its gifts. We are disappointed here because we are not meant to be completely content here. The Christian sees in this homesickness the sign of his real nature and the goal of his real striving. Men are homesick and lonely without God. It is then that they bring their disconsolate spirits and their wounded hearts and their minds filled with anguish to the mercy seat, to discover that there is no sorrow that cannot be healed by God. In the words of the psalmist:

> Happy is he that hath the God of Jacob for his help,
> Whose hope is in Jehovah his God. (Ps. 146:5.)

This is the great mission of the Church—to bring hope to despairing men. It is decreed that Christians are to look at the despair of life and be more aware of it than other men. At the same time they are to know a hope that has never been experienced by any other men. They are to look at the worst, and they are to find the best. They are to know how to be abased and how to abound.

XV

THE MIND AND THE HEART

Behold, I send you forth as sheep in the midst of wolves: be ye
therefore wise as serpents, and harmless as doves.—Matt. 10:16

A LITERARY CRITIC HAS REMARKED:

The tough-minded and the tender-minded, as William James put it—
these are the great incompatibles.

I cannot get on with tender-minded people. I like tender hearts, but
I like tough minds, those whom we used to call hard-headed. The life
of the heart thrives when people are hard-headed, while the tender-
minded play into the hands of the tough in heart. When people's heads
are soft, their hearts grow hard.

It is the tough-minded who achieve the hopes and aims of the tender
in heart.[1]

This brief comment sums up one of the great difficulties in human
life. It is the difficulty of maintaining at one and the same time the
tough mind and the soft heart. Nearly always a man has either a
soft mind and a soft heart or else a hard mind and a hard heart.
These are both wrong combinations and do unutterable harm to
him personally and, through him, to his neighbors. It is too easy to
get this matter reversed. If we are not very careful, we will allow
our minds to get mushy, soft, and fuzzy. When that happens, it is
too easy for our hearts to become hardened and unresponsive to
human needs. The demand which the good life puts upon us to be
tough-minded and tender-hearted sends us in search of help. We
do not know how to handle this matter by ourselves.

[1] Van Wyck Brooks, *Opinions of Oliver Allston* (New York: E. P. Dutton &
Co., 1941), p. 304.

The Soft Mind

Let us consider as a beginning the tragedy of the soft mind. Realistic thinking always has a bleak, austere quality about it. It is hardly too much to say that it must have a ruthless quality also, much like the surgeon's knife. It has to be willing to cut apart, putting aside all the soft flesh which stands in the way, and cut out the diseased tissue. The kind of cozy thinking which so many people do is fit only for an afternoon of gossiping over a cup of tea. Thought that is effective has to be sharp and penetrating. It is also painful, so that men will often indulge in almost any kind of fantasy and will accept almost any kind of general untruth rather than face the necessity of real thinking.

One of the most unlovely characteristics of mankind is its fear of thought or, at best, its lazy preference for comfort. It would be alarming if we realized how much of our time is spent in seeking substitutes for straight, hard thinking. We develop an amazing cleverness in postponing our problems rather than analyzing them and dealing with them. The man who counsels people in trouble is astounded at the average man's inability to face his own situation thoughtfully. It appears that after a few years of trying to run away from difficulties rather than solve them the human mind gets so soft it is no longer effective.

The soft mind can never face personal decisions. The people who indulge in this kind of thinking are always muddled personalities who are themselves a part of the terrible problem of the world. They see everything as a kind of blur. They have lost the power to penetrate sharply into the real issue at stake. They cannot admit their own mistakes, for that would be a confession of failure and weakness which they are not able to accept. Never having faced reality in any human situation, they cannot stand any sharp criticism of their own behavior. Intellectually they have learned to look at life through rose-colored glasses. They have developed a myopia which casts a golden haze over everything they observe. Intellectually they are never more than half aware, and they live in a kind of perpetual self-hypnosis.

There is little hope for this kind of person until he has learned to be tough-minded and remove every sentimental influence from his thought. We may help ourselves begin developing tough-mindedness by writing things down and facing the actual statements on a piece of paper. The fuzziness of our thought is sometimes apparent when we try to make it concrete. It is a disturbing truth that many people in the world have never used their minds in anything but a weak, timid, and emotional manner. We must think of our minds as instruments which ought to be sharp and sure instead of soft and yielding.

A great number of leaders understand this human lust for comfort and take advantage of it. They have learned that to proclaim with loud voice what the people want to hear is the surest way to win their support. The truth about the situation and the seriousness of the situation are things which these men never feel called upon to describe. Soft-minded people will resent anyone who proclaims unpleasant facts and honor the man who will tell a pleasant lie. The demagogue trades on this tendency for his own selfish advancement. The greatest enemy of truth is the number of minds which have become too soft to accept it. We become very much like the old lady who heard some of the implications of evolution explained to her and said, "God grant that it may not be true, but if it is true, God grant that not many people will hear about it." This is the attitude of the tender-minded.

There is no better illustration of the reaction of the soft-minded to truth than the story of Amos and Amaziah. It is to be noted that the king's priest did not question the facts which Amos presented, but he said to the king: "Amos hath conspired against thee in the midst of the house of Israel: the land is not able to bear all his words," and he said to Amos: "O thou seer, go, flee thou away into the land of Judah, and there eat bread, and prophesy there: but prophesy not again any more at Bethel; for it is the king's sanctuary, and it is a royal house." (Amos 7:10, 12-13.) This is the typical reaction of the soft-minded. The facts are not questioned, but because this is the king's city, it is not able to hear the message.

We want to be at ease, and so we insist on the prophet's speaking somewhere else. Yet if the king but knew, and if Amaziah but knew, it was the word of Amos which was the saving word, unpleasant as it might be; and it was the ignoring of that word which meant destruction.

In *War and Peace* Tolstoy comments on the curious reaction of people to danger when in 1812 Napoleon came closer and closer to Moscow:

At the approach of danger there are always two voices that speak with equal power in the human soul: one very reasonably tells a man to consider the nature of the danger and the means of escaping it; the other, still more reasonably, says that it is too depressing and painful to think of the danger, since it is not in man's power to foresee everything and avert the general course of events, and it is therefore better to disregard what is painful till it comes, and to think about what is pleasant. . . . It was long since people had been as gay in Moscow as that year.

Public thinking is not usually characterized by toughness.

Chancellor Robert M. Hutchins of Chicago University described the report of the President's Commission on Education as a muddled-up belief that the need is for more money and more courses, as if the vices of American education could be turned into virtues by making them larger. His comment was, "Its heart is in the right place; its head does not work very well." That comment is to the point in so many of the things we do. Unfortunately all of the virtue which might be ours because our hearts are in the right place becomes a destructive thing to us when our heads are soft.

In the opinion of many people a religious man is one who has a soft mind. They regard him as one who will believe anything and think well of the worst. In the name of being realistic, hard-hearted men criticize the Christian as a dupe and a fool. But there was no more realistic thinker in the first century than Jesus. There is no more tough-minded way of life than Christianity. If the Christian counsels mercy and good will, it is not because he is soft but because he is realistic. Compared to the toughness of the Christian way the militarist is a sentimental simpleton. The world has gone wrong by following the soft stupidity of force rather than choosing the tough and difficult path of love.

The Tough Mind

We must come to the realization that life demands a tough mind. Much of our foolishness is covered with an emotional haze and a sentimental appeal. Whenever one who is acquainted with floral costs goes to a funeral, he is impressed with the amount of money that has been spent to send flowers as a symbol of respect for the deceased. Do we dare consider how much more good we might do for men if we should spend that money for medical research to prevent untimely funerals? The Medical Memorial Fund discovered that we spend twenty dollars for flowers for every one dollar we spend in medical research. This is a place where we should cut through the softness of our thinking to see the reality of our sentimental crime. It is in the same category as the Russian empress who wept over a play while her coachman froze to death as he waited for her outside.

Science, which has accomplished so much and become so significant in our way of living, has achieved its victory through tough-mindedness. Its method is to accept nothing on trust that can be experimented with and tested. It is unwilling to say that because a thing is hallowed by age, it needs to be respected by the contemporary generation. It is not afraid to prove that grandfather may have been wrong, nice a man as he was. It will not regard anything as sacrosanct simply because it is old and full of pleasant memories. Its method is the unsentimental one of discovering what actually happens under certain situations. The man whose mind is not able to follow this very tough and direct procedure must make up his mind that he can never be a scientist.

Yet this method has made tremendous accomplishments. If its discoveries have often been prostituted for the cause of war and private gain, it is also true that this method has proved to be of the greatest service to mankind in discovering the causes of diseases and their cures. The tough methods of science, dedicated to the good goals of humanity, represent one of the most helpful possibilities in our modern world. We criticize science for its secular pride, but we do not criticize it for the method it has used. That method stands vindicated for all the world to see.

The glory of science, then, is the glory of realistic thinking. It is the glory of a tough mind. It is a symbol of clean, clear accomplishment in a world of muddy thinking and uncertainty. It reveals what men may hope to accomplish when they are no longer afraid to be unyielding in their thinking. Ancient proverbs, by exerting too much emotional power, raise effective barriers before a better world. Albert Einstein said when asked the secret of his success, "I challenged an axiom." For the tough-minded nothing is to be accepted in blind trustfulness if it is possible to subject it to the method of science.

It should be apparent to us that a similar approach in other fields would attain some of the results which we so desperately need. If only in our international relationships we could be as tough-minded as we are when dealing with the elements. If men were willing to forget their prejudices and their age-old worship of a dead past, how quickly the nations of the world could do the essential thing in establishing peace for us all. It is precisely because in these fields we are not tough-minded, but only hard-hearted, that we go wrong. The problems before us are not unsolvable. We are oftentimes able to define the answer. But we cannot bring ourselves to fearlessly pursue the matter to its ultimate conclusion and adjust our lives to what our minds have told us is truth. In social situations without number we continue to muddle along without finding an answer only because we will not face these situations as realistically as scientists. There seems to be a strange quirk in human nature which makes it shy away from straight thinking when it has to do with personalities. We believe half-truths about ourselves and pretend that we are different from what we are.

But after having looked at the failures in living, let us look at the successes and ask ourselves what they had that the failures did not have and what they did that the failures did not do. We are impressed with the fact that well-adjusted people are those who have learned a simple but profound honesty. That is, they have managed to escape the temptation of wishful thinking. They have learned how to analyze themselves objectively, and in their imagination they observe their behavior from the viewpoint of other people. It is amazing how many of our habits would irritate us beyond endurance if practiced by our close associates. Five minutes of honest analysis would reveal that fact to us. The Golden Rule is oil on the troubled waters of social relations, but the people who practice it have first learned the hard discipline of seeing themselves as others see them.

The tough-minded learn from their failures and are made stronger by their mistakes. How disarming are these people who have learned how to say simply and easily, "I was wrong. I made a blunder." But this is not easy to do, as is apparent from the relatively few people who can do it. Yet when a man has learned how to cut through his own pride and egotism and look objectively at his part in a disaster, he has learned the first difficult lesson in living with grace. The well-adjusted are tough-minded.

> Your little hands,
>   Your little feet,
> Your little mouth—
>   Oh, God, how sweet!
>
> Your little nose,
>   Your little ears,
> Your eyes, that shed
>   Such little tears!
>
> Your little voice,
>   So soft and kind;
> Your little soul,
>   Your little mind! [2]

[2] Samuel Hoffenstein, "Your Little Hands," Reprinted by permission of Liveright Publishing Corp.

Ah yes! It is nice to have sweetness and beauty in people, but when at the same time these virtues are accompanied by soft little minds, then all the sweetness is weakness and all the beauty is futile.

The Hard Heart

But if our need is for a tough mind, there is no place in great living for the hard heart. For when the heart becomes hard, we are shut off from love, which, as Henry Drummond said, is the greatest thing in the world. The heart that has become cynical and tough is no longer able to respond to the free gift of love. Thus it is not able to return that love, and it becomes the producing center of bitterness and disappointment. For better than the riches of the world is the love of men. Better than the wielding of power is the ability to draw devotion from another. When a man's heart gets hard, it does not lead him into joy but keeps him outside the warmth of affection.

It is the hard heart which prevents a man from having friends. Such a one has only acquaintances, people whom he meets in a shallow way. In spite of all the people he may know he comes to the realization someday that not one of them really cares for him because of himself. All of this, of course, is his own tragedy and his own fault. Friendship is a thing of the heart, and when the heart has a crust around it, friendship cannot enter. The person who is too trusting will sometimes be deceived. Yet the risk is worth taking, and even if at times we are misled and fooled, it is still worth it. Much better it is for the cry of need to penetrate into our hearts than for us to protect ourselves by hardening our hearts.

It is the hard heart that shuts us off from God. That is the reason Jesus attacked all those influences which make men insensitive. He was distressed by the hatred of a man for another man because that made the heart so hard God would not force his way into it. He was suspicious of riches because of their tendency to destroy human sympathy for the unfortunate. He hurled his denunciations against moral pride because it was this moral pride which separated men instead of uniting them.

We Christians do not believe that anything can shut us off from God except ourselves. We are aware of a God who will persistently seek us no matter what we do or where we go. Yet the man who begins to think of other men as means to an end soon discovers that he no longer has any sense of God's presence with him. The Christian is more concerned about this than he is about personal success. He knows that as he thinks in his heart, so is he. Every experience of life which he allows to make him bitter and cynical is a bad experience for him because it is a barrier to God. This is the reason hatred of another is always more devastating in its effect upon the hater than on the hated. This is why Jesus always counsels forgiveness and urges a willingness to be wronged rather than seek revenge. It is because the desires for hatred and vengeance are things which harden the hearts of men. They are walls raised against God himself.

To keep our hearts tender we should learn to like the right things and dislike the wrong things. The worship of mere bigness ultimately leads to the worship of big nations and big power. We do not want war, we say, but what has happened to us through the years is the imperceptible growth of a terrible fascination for the things which make war inevitable. The heart that has not grown hard still has a place for the small things, the weak things, and the kind things. But when men have learned to despise such as these in favor of the brutal and the massive, they are willing to sacrifice the lives of children and men in order to attain big things which they so deeply admire. It is then they become the worshipers of the kind of men whose appeal is to their soft minds and their hardened hearts.

The Tender Heart

The gospel demands the heart that is tender and the mind that is tough. Jesus summed it up in these words, "Behold, I send you forth as sheep in the midst of wolves: be ye therefore wise as serpents, and harmless as doves." (Matt. 10:16.) It may be a little difficult to imagine the serpent and the dove as characteristic of the same person, but this is what Jesus expects of us. We are to be wise and realistic and at the same time gentle and sympathetic.

There is a place for emotion, but there is also a place for clear thought. Whenever we endeavor to deal with a problem emotionally instead of factually, the outcome cannot be a happy one. It is too bad that there are so many religious people who seem to assume that every matter is to be decided in terms of feeling instead of in terms of fact. There is no solution for any of our problems, personal or social, until first of all we are sure we know the facts underlying them. To ferret out these facts oftentimes demands a tough, ruthless thought process.

There are times when we must be aware that men need understanding and not condemnation. There is a place for the tender heart to enter into sympathy with another rather than to stand back and objectively condemn that person. Again we see in Jesus the model we need to follow. Whenever he was attacking a group or a system that stood for the exploitation of men, how hard-minded he could be. How bitter his denunciation when he was in the presence of someone who had been more anxious for acclaim than for mercy. But how tender was his heart as he offered forgiveness rather than punishment to the person who had been more sinned against than sinning.

To find the balance in my life and yours seems to be an impossibility. In fact, our whole nature is so complex that we have difficulty in understanding it. There is no more certain sign of the shallowness of much modern psychology than its attempt to explain human life by a simple proposition. Yet over against this complexity which is true of all of us is a kind of simplicity which God gives us. A French peasant had a custom of sitting quietly for a long time in church at the end of his day's toil. When a priest asked him what he prayed for, he answered, "Oh, I just look up at Him and He looks down at me." The answer to the complexity of our life is to be found in God. When we look up at him and he looks down at us, he resolves these conflicts within our hearts. But it is only out of the experience of prayer and devotion that the balances of life are kept. For the gift of the tough mind and the tender heart has to be bestowed upon us from above. If we are left to the mercy of the world, the heart will become hard and the mind will go soft.

On December 4, 1789, Benjamin Franklin wrote to David Hartley: "God grant, that not only the Love of Liberty, but a thorough Knowledge of the Rights of Man, may pervade all the Nations of the Earth, so that a Philosopher may set his Foot any where on its Surface, and say, 'This is my Country.'" Franklin was profound enough to see that the good society would be a combination of love and knowledge. Which is to say the Kingdom demands that its citizens should possess the soft heart of the dove and the tough mind of the serpent.

XVI

REST AND SPUR

There remaineth therefore a sabbath rest for the people of God.
           —Heb. 4:9
Ye therefore shall be perfect.   —Matt. 5:48

A GREAT NUMBER OF PEOPLE ASSUME THAT CHRISTIANITY WILL GIVE them a permanent resting place and a constant peace. They become Christians with the idea of settling down somewhere and having their burdens eased. Their disillusionment begins when they discover that the gospel promises no permanent resting place. In fact it often seems just the opposite from rest. It is the spur which demands they shall move on higher than they intended to go and strive for a perfection beyond a man's reasonable expectation of attainment.

The gospel is true to life, and this is the way life treats us. It has within it a terrible demand that we shall grow or die. It seems to be more concerned with the expansion of our life and the enlargement of our vision than it is to provide for us a resting place. Life demands that men either move forward or be left behind and forgotten. Life seems to be bent on breaking the shell of the protections we are at such pains to create, and opening us up to the dangers of development. Christianity does the same thing for us, and any interpretation of it which leaves this out is a snare and a delusion. There is a rest in Christianity, but it is not the rest of ignoble ease, and it is experienced only when we have at last accepted it as a spur.

A SENSE OF THE ETERNAL

We are wrong, however, if we do not understand that there is a restfulness about Christianity which is one of the most comforting things in the world. The gospel has a great sense of the eternal, which it brings to bear upon our little hurried worries. A pagan has to rush through to his success because he feels if he does not get it now, he will not get it at all. The materialist has to have the profit shown him this moment, and if it looks as if he would have to wait, his response is restlessness and rebellion. There is in the eternal sense of the gospel something of the quietness that comes to men who learn the peace which nature seems to know. If the sense of the eternal makes us seem to be very small in our own eyes, it also makes us able to see things in clearer perspective and to find calmness amid the troubled hurry of our contemporary life.

The pagan philosophy has been beautifully presented in Omar Khayyám's *Rubaiyat*. Remember his lines:

> Some for the Glories of this World; and some
> Sigh for the Prophet's Paradise to come;
>   Ah, take the Cash, and let the Credit go,
> Nor heed the rumble of a distant Drum!

This kind of thought appeals to a generation that has lost its faith. Yet if we accept that philosophy and practice it, what then? We discover that it is self-defeating. Its promises cannot be fulfilled. It is the philosophy of the animal, but it cannot be the philosophy of a man. Men with their eternal sense of time and value cannot drug themselves into a state of accepting the joy of a passing moment as satisfying forever.

The Christian can wait because he is aware that the real issues of his life can never be decided just this moment or the next one. The issues of human life are continual and eternal. Whenever men have a firm hold on God, they are less dependent on time. Whenever the eternal breaks into a human life, the result is a sense of security that brings restfulness to tired spirits. This is the rest of patience. It is always the impatient man who wears out first, and the man who cannot afford to wait is the poorest of men. The

Psalms constantly called this to the attention of their faithless contemporaries. They told how men might slow their hurried pace and rest in the confidence that God was God and his reality made time significant but not ultimate. Whenever we come to believe that this particular moment is the only moment and what happens to us individually is decisive for mankind, it is good for us to remember the words of the ninetieth psalm:

> For a thousand years in thy sight
> Are but as yesterday when it is past,
> And as a watch in the night.

By giving us the broad view and setting our lives against the background of God the Christian gospel brings to men a rest their troubled spirits so deeply need.

A woman carrying a heavy suitcase managed to catch a crowded streetcar. When she was safely aboard, the conductor noticed that she stood in the aisle clinging tightly to the suitcase. Finally he said to her, "Lady, you can put your suitcase down now. The car will carry it for you." This is what happens to the religious man. He puts his burdens down on the eternal power of the Almighty, for he has come to know that it will carry him and his burden as well. It brings him rest and new strength to know that "underneath are the everlasting arms."

The quality of confidence is one of the sure signs of real Christianity. The man who professes to be a Christian and then lives a life controlled by a nervous uncertainty shows that his profession is a false one. We do not have to carry our religion or go about with a theological chip on our shoulders. We are rather like men whose souls are still with the quietness of the everlasting hills. The gospel saves a man from being unduly irritated by the actions of the wicked. A Christian learns to obey the command of the psalm:

> Rest in the Lord, and wait patiently for him:
> Fret not thyself because of him who prospereth in his way,
> Because of the man who bringeth wicked devices to pass. (37:7.)

The Gospel as Conservative

It is true also that the gospel is in a sense a conservative force. This is to say that it has a very deep respect for spiritual values. It does not believe for one moment that we can ever afford to divorce ourselves from them. It is too deeply aware of how their roots always go back to long-dead generations and how every present generation is dependent upon the great and painful sacrifice of its fathers. We are always in danger of letting the real accomplishments of the ages pass out of our grasp because we despise everything that is old. The true conservative is one who knows that to maintain its inheritance is one of the chief obligations and duties of any generation.

But this conservatism is also one of the most difficult things to practice. The sacrifices of our fathers, which gave us freedom and equality, can be lost in a very short time whenever we forget their significance for one moment. A deadening familiarity leads to contempt, and men can easily be influenced to prefer a cheap and flashy newness over a tried and true reality without glamour. In a day of fads anything that goes back farther than this morning is disregarded. Religion always insists that we must conserve and be loyal to the real accomplishments of yesterday. Christians are never impressed by talk of a new morality, for they do not believe there is any such thing. There are only new adaptations of old laws. There are only fresh applications of eternal principles. If there is progress in the spiritual realm, it is not discernible to human minds.

The gospel is conservative because it does not believe that change is automatically progress. Change is sometimes a reversal of the progressive process. Change is necessary in order that things may grow and develop, but it is also possible for a people to become so enamored with the idea of change that they worship it as an end in itself. This is the danger for America in our time, and it has become too characteristic of our Western civilization.

Our modern industrial society creates a feverish desire to possess the latest models. It gives the new style too much authority. Cars have to be changed every year in order that customers will be dissatisfied with the old and want the new. No one can ever claim justly that merely because the style of a car has been changed it has necessarily been made better. Clothing styles are varied from year to year in order that women will be unhappy with the old and buy the new. This has become so necessary for big business and mass production that we sometimes let the same spirit enter into our thinking regarding moral values. We want the startling and the spectacular. We like an old philosophy only if it is dressed up in sophisticated terms and sold to men through mass production methods. Against this restlessness the gospel oftentimes seems to be old-fashioned.

Christianity does not believe that life necessarily has to go up; it can go down. There have been times when we have gone back, and sometimes we have betrayed the progress made by our fathers. Thinking we were by-passing our ancestors, we followed paths which led us backward instead of going on from the place where they had left off. When a man begins to look at things from the standpoint of the eternal, he is not nearly so impressed with what his contemporaries are calling progress. When men begin to measure their values not in terms of years but in terms of the centuries, they are sometimes surprised to see that the greatest things which they have are very old things indeed.

A magazine article described the kind of person that knows no rest and no calm: "There is hardly a more lovable or more irritating woman in existence. She is all yearning and no peace, all travel and no arrival, and the whole trip a constant fuss with the baggage and wonder if some other route might not have been better." [1] Into the midst of such a restless spirit comes Christianity with its eternal vision and its insistence on the validity and importance of the values which never change.

It is common for men to assume that the liberal spirit means an ignoring of the past and that a conservative is another name for a reactionary. No true liberal is so foolish as to assume that wisdom

[1] Jeanne Singer, "One Woman's Hat," Harper's Magazine, May, 1946, p. 398.

began with him, and a true conservative knows that he is the guardian of living values. No discipline helps a man or a generation to keep the past and the present in their right relationship like the Christian faith. It is rest and a spur.

CHRISTIANITY AND THE STATUS QUO

If we should stop here, however, and insist that the gospel is only a conservative viewpoint and a conservative influence in the world, we would do it a grave injustice. We need to see that, along with these other characteristics, Christianity never is willing to worship the *status quo*. If it is a conservative force in a generation, it is always a revolutionary force as well. There is enough dynamite in the teachings of Jesus to blow any social system apart if they are taken seriously. Real Christianity has always been a dangerous thing in the lives of its adherents and in the life of a society.

Over and against every social institution the gospel always holds the reality of the Kingdom of God. Because no other institution ever comes near to measuring up to the demands of the Kingdom, the gospel is a spur to each man who takes the Kingdom seriously. It demands that he shall somehow bring into the light of the Kingdom of God every institution of which he is a part. That means the Christian is always a critic of the way things are because he knows that he has been called to make them better. He is a critic of every institution and a spur to every good striving.

Over and against the classes of society which are so firmly established and so comfortably arranged the gospel proclaims the demands of brotherhood. The fortunate classes of a society are never ready to give up their privileges and are never anxious to have ideas spread throughout the masses that will make them more unhappy and dissatisfied than they are. The revolt of the peasants in Martin Luther's time was more than he had bargained for and a very serious embarrassment to him. But that is the way this gospel of ours is. Give it an inch, and it takes a mile. Once it is given a chance to run loose in the lives and thoughts of men, they are never satisfied again with the relationship of master and slave. Christianity always has the disturbing effect of making us feel that all men are brothers and brotherhood should be the rule of life.

We can grow quite content with our human justice, even though it is far from perfect, because we tend to think that if we go through the motions, we make a society stable. It may be quite true that the wealthy man has an advantage over the poor man. It may be quite true that in the courts justice is defined by the whipped-up emotions of the community. With these limitations most men may be content. But the Christian has the sense of God's justice, which is even-handed and uninfluenced by circumstances. Until our human justice makes some real attempt to bring itself into alignment with God's justice, the Christian must be a spur and a challenge to his society.

All of this seems very revolutionary and the exact opposite of conservatism. Yet in a strange way the revolutionary aspect of the gospel grows out of its conservative nature. For if Christians demand change and improvement, it is precisely because they are so old-fashioned as to believe in the God of their fathers, who demands that our ways shall be brought into closer approximation to his ways. Christianity may be regarded by many as something which turns the world upside down. But that is because the real world, whose order was established before the hills stood, is their model. The Christian may appear as a radical to his contemporaries, but his radicalism is simply his sense of God's changeless principles, upon which all human society must stand if it is to endure.

Christianity, therefore, is oftentimes regarded as a very dangerous element in human life. It is so regarded by tyrants and by every powerful group who believe that the *status quo* should not be challenged. It gives men wild and strange ideas about their status and their nature. It asks embarrassing questions about special privilege. Where did these privileges come from? Who earned them? Why does this particular group have them instead of the other group? What do these favored ones contribute in return for their special privileges? All of this makes the gospel appear to many a man as a most discomforting and troublesome affair.

The truth is that the Christian marches to a different music from his contemporaries. They hear the band playing the march of success. They stay in line with their superiors. They keep in step with the ethics of the street. But the Christian marches to the music of God. He marches in the procession of Christ. His music is the music of the Kingdom. Because this is a different kind of marching from that of so many men, he is often out of step with them and hence a disturbing factor according to their point of view. Christianity is aware of the constant tension between the old and the new, and it has no faith in a sacred equilibrium which ends in an atrophy and a withering.

Dorothy Thompson one time summed up this double nature of life when she said, "Without change there can be no growth. But without tradition there can be no civilization." New branches must come forth, it is true. Every year they must come forth, and we shall learn to expect them. But we shall also know that the new branches have to come out of the old tree whose roots go back down through the centuries and are nourished by visions of men long ago dead. Precisely because Christianity is a spur to men and a challenge to the *status quo*, it also provides for them rest and calm, as they align their lives, not with the merely comfortable, but with the right.

We Are Pilgrims

Finally it needs to be said that Christianity sees men as pilgrims in the world. We are travelers on our way to a place beyond our sight. We always sleep in a foreign land at the close of every day. Our rest must come from the assurance that we are on the march and that we are going somewhere we ought to go. Any other confidence than this is stagnation. Our religion is a part of us, and yet it is always beyond us. It is the experience upon which we stand and also something to be experienced in some far tomorrow. It is a fact and a possibility. Without it life has no meaning, and yet it is itself beyond our complete comprehension. It is something we possess and something beyond our reach. Until we face this seeming contradictory nature of our faith, we cannot understand it, and we cannot understand ourselves. We must come to the realization that

179

somehow the rest of the gospel lies in the fact that the gospel is a spur.

Christianity refuses to let men settle down. As long as we are Christians, we are moving—strangers here but going toward a home in heaven which is our destination. Just when we think we are safe and can stop for a while, we hear the trumpet call and must be on our way again. Because men grow weary with boredom and because they are tired by the nervousness of their life, they discover that this sense of progress, this sense of being pilgrims, is a satisfaction to them. By eliminating the stagnation of boredom it keeps us alert, strong, and rested.

If the old institutions cannot accept the new life, then men are forced to build new ones. For nothing must stand in the way of that clarion call which comes to men from Christ, demanding a better and a greater life. Every obstacle seems to be a kind of temptation which we are to overcome. To the Christian the obstacle becomes a challenge and a spur. To accept anything made by men as of an ultimate nature is the most fatal of mistakes. For this is to assume that men are of the earth only. Their institutions, created by their own hands, become the objects of an uncritical loyalty. This is idolatry.

By understanding that we are pilgrims on the road of life we will not expect to gather too many possessions which can be held permanently. We know all these things pass, and the important thing is that we should get on and follow the path God has set for us. This keeps things in their proper place. The Oregon Trail was lined with superfluous possessions discarded by the American pioneers. The trail soon revealed what was essential. So when men conceive their lives as permanently established in the world, their earthly treasures become too important. But when they learn that human life is a pilgrimage, the luxuries can be separated from the necessities.

Yet, while we are always moving on, we are always at home. To no strange place do we go, but to our own land and to our own people. With enough homesickness in our hearts to make us dissatisfied with things as they are we keep moving toward that freedom which we can find only in the service of our Lord. Out of our traveling comes the rest we need. It is only when we settle down that our weariness becomes unbearable.

We are to have faith enough in God to live each day sufficient unto itself. Looking too far ahead overwhelms us with the number of obstacles in the way. Fearful of the difficulties, we will be tempted to call off the journey. But it is wonderful how God smooths the way when we take life a day at a time. Looking back, we are astounded at the way we have been strengthened and protected. How many apprehensions were ghosts raised by our own timidity! This is the experience of the Christian who feels the spur of the gospel urging him forward. A strange new power is released in his life which brings him strength enough to endure with joy.

Or, to put it in a different way, a man erected a tombstone in memory of his wife on the banks of the James River. On the stone he cut these words: "She touched the soil of Virginia with her little foot, and the wilderness became a home." So it is that while God oftentimes sends us into the wilderness to wander until we discover the promised land, his presence there makes the wilderness a home to our souls. The gospel is a spur to men, but it is also a rest. It has the divine magic to bring us rest by redeeming us from the slavery of an unworthy contentment.

XVII

NECESSITY AND FREEDOM

For necessity is laid upon me.   —I Cor. 9:16
If therefore the Son shall make you free, ye shall be free indeed.
                                                  —John 8:36

ONE OF THE DISASTROUS THINGS MAN CAN DO IS TO CONFUSE NE-
cessity and freedom. There is a realm in which we have no choice,
and we must adjust ourselves to things as they are. A refusal to do
that can only result in failure. On the other hand there is the realm
of human freedom, where we must never allow external compulsions
to enter. The oft-quoted prayer of Reinhold Niebuhr is one which
each man would do well to repeat many times: "God grant me the
serenity to accept the things I cannot change, the courage to change
the things I can, and the wisdom to know the difference."

We have tried in our time to solve the problems of life by assuming that any man can do anything he really desires to do. This idea
has brought much unhappiness to many young people because it is
utter nonsense. To tell a boy or a girl he should expect to attain anything he has in mind is to practice cruelty. There are the limitations
which God has put upon us in the way of gifts and abilities. Whenever we begin to educate for success only and to assume that every
person is going to become the president of the United States, we are
creating neuroses, and we are damaging human souls. A contemporary cartoon showed a young father telephoning a newspaper on
the birth of his son and saying, "You give plenty of space when a
famous man dies. Why can't you give some space when a famous
man is born?" That is a fine feeling for a parent to have, but it is a

dangerous foundation for a philosophy of life. There ought to be a larger place in our thinking and in the training of our youth for the acceptance of the way things are and the ability to adjust our lives to inevitabilities.

At the same time we need to tell young people a good deal about the essential freedoms and their duty to defend those freedoms at all costs. There is no safety for any democracy until its citizens have come to understand that there is a certain line beyond which they must allow no external force to go. All of this is best understood by the gospel, which assumes that if a man is to be free, he must also be a slave to the things which make for freedom. All of this is made clear when Paul can say that necessity is laid upon him, and at the same time he can insist on the freedom of men in Christ. The Fourth Gospel speaks of slavery to sin and then adds: "If therefore the Son shall make you free, ye shall be free indeed." (8:36.)

THE WORLD OF PURPOSE

The Christian begins with the assumption that the world in which he lives reveals order and purpose. He will not accept—for indeed he cannot accept—the feeling that he lives in a madhouse. The idea of creation by chance and directionless drifting is not a reasonable one, and even the secularist who studies the physical universe with unprejudiced eyes is driven to a confession of faith in some purpose which he may not be able to define with any clearness, but which has left unmistakable traces.

The world as the result of blind chaos demands more naïve belief and more credulity than an intelligent man can give it. That things have happened simply because they have happened goes against all of our experience in every other realm of life. When we begin to study the laws of chance, we begin to see they make it impossible for us to assume an orderless beginning of the world. It is not too much to say today that this materialist point of view and this nonteleological theory has less and less standing in the minds of thoughtful people. We may not agree at all as to the meaning of the

183

world's purpose or its origin. But there are very few people who can look at the world without saying that somewhere, somehow, at the beginning of the whole process there was a purpose.

That very outstanding book *Human Destiny*, written by the late internationally known French scientist Lecomte duNoüy, has dealt with this problem with clearness and conviction. In the introduction the author stated very clearly a conclusion and a thesis: "The purpose of this book is to examine critically the scientific capital accumulated by man, and to derive therefrom logical and rational consequences. We shall see that these consequences lead inevitably to the idea of God." [1] It would seem that the scientific world comes closer and closer to the Christian interpretation of things when it declares that life reveals a world with a meaning. This, of course, intimates that by the very nature of things there is a kind of necessity in the world.

But even if physical nature did not reveal this truth, human nature certainly reveals it. That is to say that nobody acts as if the world were purposeless and life were meaningless. Even the individual who proclaims in positive tone that, so far as he is concerned, life means nothing continues to live as if he believed it did. His behavior is more convincing than his talk, and it is in the way he lives that we discover his real faith.

This, I think, can be illustrated very clearly by the example of the orthodox Communist. On the one hand he will assert the inevitable dialectical movement of history through the liquidation of the capitalist class to the dictatorship of the proletariat on to its predestined end in the classless state. This, he will tell us, has to be and must be. There is no choice involved and there is no freedom in it. It is a kind of predestination in the material realm which nothing can affect or change. But at the same time he grows very indignant at the wickedness of capitalist society. He cannot find words bitter enough to attack the middle class in a democracy. Yet if his theory is right, progress is possible only through the tension and the strug-

[1] (New York: Longmans, Green & Co., 1947), p. xvi.

gle of capitalism on the one hand and Communism on the other. Why should he become indignant at the evil of the capitalist? According to this theory the capitalist is a pawn in the whole process, and an essential one if the necessary results are to be achieved. The plot has been constructed by conditions beyond human control, and each man must inevitably play his part in that drama. Why become so morally indignant, therefore, at the man who has been condemned to play the part of the villain? The answer is that the orthodox Communist, like everybody else, lives differently from his talk. He does not believe that these things are inevitable, but he assumes that men have choices and that sometimes they make evil choices. He may deny it, but he lives on the basis of a bourgeois morality.

There are Christians who will say that nothing can be done about making the world better. They believe the world is doomed to get worse and worse until the second coming of Christ. They will interpret the events of the contemporary situation so as to show that the Lord's coming is very near. When that happens, they tell us, the world is to be destroyed, and the new kingdom is to be established. But until that happens, there is no point in trying to make life better. That, at least, is the theory. Yet how do these people live? They live like every other Christian lives, doing their best to improve life for every suffering brother. They cannot escape the conviction that they are called upon to play their part as if their behavior would make a real difference. We may talk about the blind necessities of processes and of life, but there is something in humanity which prevents our living like that.

Professor Alfred North Whitehead one time commented on this tendency to deny theory by practice. Speaking of scientists who claimed that human life was without cause or goal, he said, "Scientists who spend their life with the purpose of proving that it is purposeless constitute an interesting subject of study." We cannot escape the feeling that the world has significance. Men are best engaged when they seek patiently and persistently to comprehend its purpose and learn to co-operate with it.

The Inexorables

Yet there are the inexorables of experience which we cannot escape, and regarding which we have no choice. Necessity is laid upon us very often, and the only intelligent reaction we can make is to accept it with grace. Much of the unhappiness of the world is due to a failure to understand this. A great deal of the worry which weakens men is simply a refusal to face facts which must be accepted. But as long as they refuse to do that, they will fuss and fret about possibilities which really do not exist. Amazingly enough, when a man has adjusted himself to what may seem to him to be the worst, the burden is taken from his shoulders, and he discovers that he can always endure whatever has to be endured.

Sooner or later a society must come to terms with this truth also. We cannot do as we like in dealing with our social problems. It is not possible for us to play fast and loose with prices, for example. Government control and government interference is always necessary in a complicated society, but let us not be so foolish as to assume that therefore we can go contrary to the necessities laid upon us by economic principles. Back of the downfall of civilizations there is always an unwillingness to face the reality of unchangeable necessities. A careful analysis of the way things are and the way things have to be is always the beginning of a successful adjustment to life.

We see this clearly in the realm of science. A scientific generation should have learned the truth of this in ordering its social life. No scientist feels badly used or objects because a particular experiment he has tried did not work out. He does not go around complaining because this law is not the way he would like to have it be. He may feel a human disappointment when a beautiful theory is slaughtered by a stubborn fact. But he knows that the one thing he must do above everything else is to accept these laws as they are and learn how, within the limitations of his freedom, to use them to help him create what he would like to have. So far as he can tell, there is no magic formula that will change ordinary materials into

186

gold. The vain dream of the old alchemist was characteristic of men who still hoped they might find an effortless way to wealth and an easy path to the accomplishment of all their desires. The scientist today is a man who asks for nothing of the kind, nor does he expect it. He studies to learn what the facts seem to mean. Once those things are known, he understands his job is the use of the inevitable realities and the adjustment of his efforts to them.

This same truth should be understood in the moral and spiritual realm. This is the place where men cry out in desperation against the way things are. In the realm of the spirit many people spend their time hammering their heads against the stone walls of reality. Until a man understands that here too it is not all freedom, but it is sometimes necessity, he is not prepared to live intelligently. To understand the difference between what can be changed and what can't be changed is the beginning of wisdom, and we may say also it is the beginning of happiness.

Charles Clayton Morrison uses a very helpful picture in describing this situation. He says we are like passengers on a ship. We are allowed to exercise a good deal of freedom on board that ship. We can decide to eat or not to eat, to play or not to play, to sit on deck or stay in the lounge. We may read or we may gamble during the days and the nights. But so far as the ship itself is concerned, we cannot decide which way it will go or how fast it will go or just when it will arrive at its destination. Our freedom is to be thought of within the limitations of the ship. Many things will happen to us which we did not ask for and which we really do not like.

FREEDOM OF THE CHRISTIAN

Yet the experience of the apostle Paul was a great release and fulfillment. It was an experience which every Christian discovers in his religion. Whenever human liberty is denied, someone like Paul comes along and proclaims that it is God's will that men shall be free. They shall be free through his service. As Martin Luther put it in his *Treatise on Christian Liberty*, "The Christian man is a perfectly free lord of all, subject to none." Yet also, as he says later, "the Christian man is a perfectly dutiful servant of all, subject to all."

The Christian finds a freedom from drifting. The man lost in the woods, who discovers he has come back to exactly the place he started, is characteristic of a man who gets lost in the midst of life. The passing years find that he has come back almost to the place where he started. The goals he dreamed of achieving are as far removed as ever. It is then that he knows a final despair. It is the despair of having lost himself and failed to arrive at one single worth-while goal.

In one of his first books, entitled *Night Flight*, Antoine de Saint-Exupéry, the late French aviator and philosopher, describes the lost feeling of the aviator in the midst of the darkness. Finally catching the whisper of a radio control operator, he frantically asks him to flash the signal at the air field to learn whether or not the light he sees on the horizon is safety or a star. When the man replies that he has flashed the light, but the flier sees nothing happen, he knows that he has not found yet the light which will guide him home. The Christian with his eyes on Jesus Christ has no doubt that if he walks through the woods or flies through the darkness of the night, he can never get lost. He is free.

Professor Harold de Wolf of Boston University School of Theology tells of an experience which describes the panic of men who have no fixed point of reference. He went swimming one night in the Atlantic with a friend. The water was full of phosphorescent light, and every time a wave broke it showered the night with brilliance. He said he felt as if he were immersed in a fireworks display. Then, having gone further out than he intended, he looked up to the sky to get his bearings. But the sky was like the water—full of the spectacular confusion of the northern lights. No star was visible. Then panic took hold of him, for in all that glittering display there was no fixed reality. He started back with a helpless terror engulfing him.[2] It is this slavery of fear which has its way with us when we

[2] *The Religious Revolt Against Reason* (New York: Harper & Bros., 1949), pp. 17-18.

are lost. Freedom is knowing where we are and what we are. It is having a star to steer by. It is putting our hand into the hand of God, which is "better than light and safer than a known way."

The Christian man is free from sin. This is not to say that he can believe he will never sin again, but he now knows that sin can never be his master. He can be cleansed and forgiven. He can be free from the feeling of futility which is so characteristic of the man caught in the power of sin. He knows at last that he is engaged in a great enterprise where each must play his part with courage. He knows he will never again doubt the value of his struggle and the assurance of his victory.

He is now free to be a son of God. He has become a part of a great family which also demands that its obligations shall be fulfilled, it is true. Yet somehow in the fulfillment of those obligations is the security which means freedom to him. Men are truly free when they belong to a believing community and have accepted its obligations. For out of that experience comes the release of their energies for the best things. It is not the demands of living against which we rebel but the loneliness of the fear that comes to people who do not belong. To be brought into the divine family is to be freed from the lawlessness of the outlaw and the fear of the gang.

This spiritual calm and this psychological freedom from panic is an often repeated miracle experienced by the Christian. The disciples felt it when the storm arose on Galilee. Men who stand in danger are often amazed at the sense of God's protection which envelops them. Of one thing the Christian is sure: God hears his prayers and sets him free from the domination of terror. The freedom of the Christian man is this assurance that out of the common things and out of the spectacular crises God holds us up. For over and against the necessities of life there stands the providence of God.

FREE SLAVES

A Christian is a man who recognizes that freedom is to be found by way of commitment. He becomes in a sense a free slave. He understands the meaning of Paul's declaration that if we are to be

189

free, we have to be bound. This freedom is, in reality, a sense of dignity which God gives his children. When men do not feel adequate, they seek to escape the fear in their hearts by subscribing to a theory that no man can be free anyway since all is decided and determined. There is no use arguing against this theory, for it is the mark of a sick mind. One cannot argue people back into health. Intellectually one can make as good a case for determinism as he can for free will, for it then becomes a matter of logic and not of life. But the matter is not settled on that level. It is settled in the realm of human experience. When a man faces the problem there, he knows that he makes choices and to some extent at least is responsible for those choices. Men do not remove their fear of being inadequate by taking refuge in irresponsibility. A Christian experience is the answer to their need, and usually it is the only thing which will help them to place their insufficiency in God's hands and receive his adequacy.

The Christian is able to understand that his main problem is not lack of leadership—although that may be serious enough. Leadership grows out of the people and is a result rather than a cause. The age of faith has more leaders than it can use because each man is looking for a chance to lead. It is the age of doubt that cries out for a strong man, and it gets men like Hitler and Mussolini. Thus you have a contrary situation where the more you ask to be saved by a great leader, the less chance you have to find him, while in the time you do not need him he is always there.

The Christian knows his problems can never be solved by the passing of laws. The law can never be a substitute for character, for we are not saved by systems. The law can condemn and punish, but it does not function where a society's vital decisions are made. They are decided in the spiritual realm, which is always outside the enforceable. The Christian knows at last that he himself must find the ability to be unbound yet committed. It is the acceptance of God's necessity that makes men free.

Life for the Christian becomes a cavalcade. He knows that pleasure alone is always a dead end but that loyalty to the best is a path

190

that does not end. Over against the pagan idea that we can have freedom by escaping duty Christianity understands that we can have freedom only through obedience to our own inner voice which is the whisper of God. The pursuit of goodness is the most exciting adventure and the most satisfying experience. To have a part in the great contest of right against wrong and to be on the right side is a freeing experience because it is the fulfillment of our real desires. Christians have been called to give themselves to the one in whose service they find perfect freedom. The necessity laid upon us by God is not slavery but release.

Remember the words of Hans Denk's prayer:

O my God, how does it happen in this poor old world that Thou art so great and yet nobody finds Thee, that Thou callest so loudly and nobody hears Thee, that Thou art so near and nobody feels Thee, that Thou givest Thyself to everybody and nobody knows Thy name? Men flee from Thee and say they cannot find Thee; they turn their backs and say they cannot see Thee; they stop their ears and say they cannot hear Thee.

Is it not because we rebel against the ultimate necessity of human experience, which is to find God and be found by him? But if we should accept that truth, the confusion of the seeming conflict between necessity and freedom would be ended. In Christ the necessities of life become the road to our freedom.

XVIII

SPIRITUAL AND MATERIAL

O death, where is thy sting?   O grave, where is thy victory?
—I Cor. 15:55 (K.J.V.)
Now concerning the collection for the saints. —I Cor. 16:1

THE FIFTEENTH CHAPTER OF PAUL'S FIRST EPISTLE TO THE CORIN-
thians is one of the high points in the New Testament. In this
chapter he discusses immortality, and he brings together the Greek
and Hebrew ideas in a satisfying synthesis. At Easter, when our
thoughts are centered around the spiritual realities and life after
death, we are always turning to this great discussion of the apostle.
It takes us to the very mountaintop of experience, and it gives us a
vision that is one of the most inspiring and comforting men can
have.

If we read on in this letter, however, we discover that from that
mountaintop of spiritual vision Paul suddenly turns to about the
most prosaic thing in the world, namely, the taking of a collection.
He begins the sixteenth chapter with the words, "Now concerning
the collection." He then goes on to tell what the arrangements will
be for the collecting of the money which he is expecting the Corinthian church to contribute for the poor saints in Jerusalem. When
we read this letter at one sitting, we have the feeling that the contrast here is almost too sharp, too great. How can Paul in one
moment be thinking of the spiritual reality of life after death and
the next moment, without any hesitancy, begin to talk about
collecting money?

The answer is that the sharp differentiation is more apparent to us than it would be to him. When a man has committed his whole life to his Lord, as did Paul, there is no great contrast between what we call the spiritual things and the material things. There is little doubt that in the mind of the apostle it was no more a religious act to meditate on the meaning of immortality than it was to consider the giving of money for a good purpose. There is something about the Christian faith when it is taken as a way of life that transforms every action into a sacrament. It is fatal for Christians to lose sight of this unity, for then they go wrong. If our religion is a very spiritual thing, it must never be forgotten that it is also a very practical matter.

OTHERWORLDLINESS

There have always been those who would make Christianity completely otherworldly. They have the feeling that the gospel is too tender to touch the earth and walk in the dust. They believe that Christianity is a very aristocratic thing and should not be expected to deal with the ordinary and the commonplace. These people are a little like the Chinese scholar who saw two Christian missionaries playing tennis. He could not understand why two men would play with such intensity as to perspire in the hot sun. When they paused to change sides, he asked them if it would not be possible to hire some coolies to play this game for them. That is the feeling which many people have regarding spiritual truth. It is not fitting that it should use its muscles or be brought into contact with material things.

Back of this idea is the unconscious belief that the world is completely and hopelessly evil. There is the assumption that religion would be contaminated if it should touch life too practically. This was primarily the feeling of Buddha. He was a young prince brought up in a sensuous and lustful court. Becoming tired of that, he decided he wanted something he could not find in that atmosphere, and he was sure he must find it by despising the physical activities of the world. Finally he came to his great principle, which he called detachment. He said the way to be happy was to detach oneself from the emotions of life. He was suspicious of love because he thought it involved human desires. If a man would practice detachment until he had no desires, Buddha believed, he might then enter into Nirvana, where a man, because he wanted nothing, could be at peace.

It is very easy to see that this is something quite different from the teaching of Christianity. Jesus did not hesitate to mix in the life of men. He was no ascetic retreating from social affairs. He was in the midst of the crowds, and he was a guest in the homes of his friends. Jesus did not believe it was necessary to withdraw from the world's life to keep oneself unspotted by its stain. Our Lord looked upon the world that God had made, "and, behold, it was very good."

In this he was the great inheritor of the prophets. The prophetic tradition of Israel assumed that the world was to become the Kingdom of God. Not for them did the retreat into the monastery have any appeal. They were the most practical men dealing with the most practical problems of society. They were sure that they were never more religious than when they were uttering God's demand for justice in the social situation in which they were involved. The world might be bad and in great need of reformation, but it was not by its very nature an evil place.

If we have any doubt about this matter it would be eliminated by a great verse in the Gospel of John. In one of the most quoted verses of the whole Bible John gives us this Christian insight into the nature of the world: "For God so loved the world, that he gave his only begotten Son, that whosoever believeth on him should not perish, but have eternal life." (John 3:16.) What a wonderful thing it is that God loved the world! It makes it forever impossible for us to believe that the world is beyond redemption or beyond purity. How can we call a thing unclean which has been described as the recipient of God's love?

Whenever Christianity is regarded as essentially otherworldly, with little concern for this world, Christian truth is distorted. Apparently something very significant has been amputated, and it bleeds. One of the worst possible things any church can do is to assume its message deals only with the other world and is only incidentally concerned with this one. Lutheranism in Germany is a case in point. When the test came, it was discovered that the bravest opponents of Hitler were nearly always religious men. But the tragedy was that Hitler might never have grown powerful enough to become a serious threat to free men if the church had warned of his danger from the very beginning. The concept of politics as in a realm divorced from the church's interest was too prevalent. There was too much the feeling that there are two kingdoms, and in the earthly kingdom the political leader is to be unchallenged. Even a man like Barth, whose theology in the beginning was often regarded as having no social implications, has now confessed that this interpretation of Christianity seems to him to be a mistake. It is now apparent that the Church has a responsibility to proclaim its faith, not only as it affects the afterlife of man, but as it affects his social life here and now.

The Orthodox Church in Russia was finally regarded by many as an enemy of the common people precisely because it preached resignation to an unjust and unnecessary suffering and exploitation. A great deal of the Communist's attack on Christianity is an attack on a one-sided interpretation of it. We know that the gospel is never truly the opiate of the people and can be regarded as such only when half of it is preached and the other half neglected. A church that neglects this present life sooner or later finds the enmity of the people raised against it and has sealed its own doom. It may think that for a time, because it has political power and wealth, as the Roman Church has had in Mexico and Spain, it will be able to weather any storm that comes along. History says No. History says that the time will come when the people will rise and be free. When that happens, if they look upon the church as their enemy, the church will have to pay for its neglect. The people have an unshakable belief that an institution true to the spirit of Christ will be concerned about their plight in this world.

One of the show places of the West is Forest Lawn Cemetery in Los Angeles. No one who visits it and sees all the beauty that has been placed there can ever forget it. We cannot be anything but grateful to those who have been responsible for its creation. They have gone out of their way to avoid anything suggesting sorrow, suffering, or dying. The Crucifixion is noticeable because of its absence. Christ is always one who "smiles and loves you and me." That this is a very real part of the gospel none of us would wish to deny. But that this is all the gospel we must emphatically deny. For the Christ whom we preach is not merely one who promised mansions in his Father's house; he is also one who commanded us to take our crosses daily and follow him bravely.

THIS-WORLDLINESS

We may go clear to the other extreme and remark that there are people who make Christianity of this world only and utterly neglect its eternal meaning. If the gospel is not something entirely beyond history, neither is it something which can be confined within history. Under this category are the cults who talk about finding the key people of a community and working through them. These key people are nearly always business executives, people of wealth, people of social position. One wonders why Jesus was ever content with fishermen, publicans, and repentant sinners. Of course from the standpoint of this world Jesus was quite wrong, and these cults are quite right. If we are going to make our religion merely a matter of conformity to the mores of the present social situation, then we will be more concerned about the key people of the community than we are about the humble ones.

We have been through a period during these past years when we have tried to make a religion without anything supernatural in it. We have tried to minimize all in our faith that has to do with theology or with belief. There has been an honest belief that nothing beyond this world is significant. Only making life better for all men here and now has been considered worthy of human effort. Oftentimes the humanists have shown real devotion and a willing-

196

ness to sacrifice that the life of the common man might be improved. But something went wrong with their attempt. Men turned to earthly gods instead of to God. Well meaning as they might be, these people found themselves utterly helpless when attacked by the ruffians who had a crude but powerful faith. Our religion is concerned with this world and what goes on in it, but it is not a religion which can be confined to this world alone. It is no better to make it entirely this-worldly than it is to make it entirely other-worldly. Nor is there any profit in trying to make Christianity a service-club altruism as opposed to a spiritual discipline.

Men are not only social creatures related to each other; they are also persons related to God. Over and against man in the crowd is man who stands entirely alone in a splendid isolation from all other men. Christianity is involved in the social situation, but it has also a word about each man's destiny and his ultimate faith. If it is concerned with the collection, it is also concerned with victory over death.

A religion of this world only often finds God an interruption rather than a necessity. It puts its trust in man, and it always creates pride. Yet its final conclusion is disillusionment, as man comes to understand that in his own power he cannot enter the Kingdom of God.

How quickly the most simple questions about life lead us beyond the boundaries of this world. Nothing that really matters is capable of being explained here. Before we realize what has happened, we are beyond our depth and gazing wistfully beyond the farthest horizon. The world is not big enough for us. In spite of our comprehension of a universe bigger than our ability to accept, it is yet too small for our souls.

SPIRITUALIZING THE MATERIAL

What the gospel does is spiritualize the material things of life and give them new significance. This is nowhere more apparent than in its attitude toward the body. While the Greeks saw the physical things of life as evil in themselves, the Christian, in the words of Paul saw the human body as a temple of the Holy Spirit. This was the reason that lust became so evil in the mind of the Christian. It was evil because it was the desecration of a temple not made for lust but made for beauty. But this also is the reason asceticism is wrong according to the Christian point of view. It denies the goodness of the body and its possibilities for holiness. When John Wesley said that cleanliness is next to godliness, he was speaking of the gospel's understanding of the essential rightness of the material things of life, when properly regarded and properly used. It is the use of a thing which determines its sacredness or its secularism, and it is the spiritual use of the material which redeems it and makes it good.

For all the material things of life are to be regarded as gifts to us from God, which means that while we do not own anything, we administer material things for the Lord. This is what Christian stewardship means. It is the attitude the businessman should take toward his business. He is not asked by Christianity to give it up and to retire into seclusion; he is asked only to understand what the ultimate purpose of it is and what his own responsibility is. He is called to his ministry through his business, which is to say he must spiritualize its methods and goals.

Christianity says to each man that his lifework is to be thought of as the greatest contribution he can make to God's Kingdom. It will have none of the contrast between sacred work and secular work. Every man's work is a sacred task if it is done for the glory of God and the service of men. It is when we get our sense of values mixed up and confuse means with ends that this material world goes wrong. This is where the spiritual comes in and makes us understand that every material thing is to be used for some holy purpose and dedicated to some worth-while cause. The great danger of money is not in the money itself but in the terrible fascination which it holds for men. When they believe that in itself money has some value and significance, they have become unchristian. But when money has been spiritualized, it is the servant of the good and the builder of a better life. When a man gets to the place that he is no longer interested in what money can do but only in accumulating it, he is spiritually speaking a failure.

One of the tragic happenings since the end of the war was the suicide of John G. Winant, who had endeared himself to the British people as few of our diplomats have done. His death was regarded as a loss by England as well as by the United States, and in an editorial on his death the *Manchester Guardian* said, "It is a sad commentary on our postwar world that John Winant could not bear to live in it." So it is. Yet, bad as our world is, and discouraging as the situation seems to be, men have to live in it and deal with it and work on it. This is where the Christian has an advantage far beyond his pagan neighbor. His faith gives spiritual significance to the struggle and makes even the material things of life wonderful in their possibilities. To the taking of the collection for the poor saints of Jerusalem there is brought to bear that great vision of our victory over death. The collection then becomes the act of a creature who has an eternal destiny, and the money takes on spiritual implications. It is this experience which enables the Christian to face undismayed the most terrible situations and the most discouraging of prospects. Shining through the material is the light of eternity which transforms our life here into a new pattern.

Materializing the Spiritual

Now we would have only one side of the picture if we did not understand that while Christianity spiritualizes the material, it also materializes the spiritual. It is not content to leave things hanging in the air. It demands that we shall take these impulses within us and do something about them in terms of practical activity here and now. The difficulty with so many spiritually minded people is that they assume religion to be a matter of contemplation and meditation only. The gospel is never content with our high ideals until we have embodied them in acts. The task is to take the great spiritual insights of the gospel and give those unseen things a body. We become for those ideals hands to strike with and feet to march on. Christ is never content with disciples only saying, "Lord Lord."

He is not pleased with followers who hear the sayings and do them not.

There is nothing in our human experience that does not have implications far beyond itself, if we have eyes to see. The most commonplace matter has something within it that is both infinite and urgent. A faithless generation will miss this completely and confine its religion to the mysterious and the unknown. But the Christ is never content with disciples only saying, "Lord, Lord." the unseen Companion and seeing the marks of the eternal God.

The national policies of the world seem bent on war. We talk about peace a great deal, but we accept the things which result in war. When it comes to actually embodying peace principles, we say it is impossible. Strangely enough, the idea of the impossible is only a challenge to us in the physical realm. It was said that when the United States built the Panama Canal, she called to that task men who specialized in doing the impossible. However, when it comes to setting the world on a different basis or experimenting with a new attitude, we are too quick to say it cannot be done. We are in desperate need of groups who are willing to embody the ideals of peace and live the commands of the gospel which will bring peace. One of the most distressing sights to observe is the number of politicians who talk glibly about Christianity, and even quote the Sermon on the Mount, yet in their own political careers have done nothing to embody those principles in their actual participation in government. We have stressed too much this business of spiritualizing the material. We have neglected the other side of the picture, which is to give visible reality to the things of the spirit.

No man ought to feel an impulse in his life to be a greater man without doing something about it. It may be quite harmful to attend church week after week and be inspired, and then let that inspiration die shortly after the service ends. The man lifted to the presence of God ought to resolve that before the next Sabbath comes around he will do at least one thing to materialize his inspiration. This is what Paul was doing for the Corinthian Christians. He had lifted their minds to the world beyond and to the eternal destiny which was theirs. Then, lest they should simply ponder that matter for a little while and forget it, he was bringing them something which they must do then to show their worthiness to be called the sons of God. "Now concerning the collection," he says. He was trying to make them understand that from the mountaintops Christians must always come down into the town, there to make real the vision which they have received.

"Christianity," as the late Archbishop of Canterbury said, "is the most avowedly materialistic of all the great religions." [1] It does not hesitate to proclaim that "the Word became flesh." It does not deny the reality of the material, and it never tries to ignore it. Yet the contemporary Christian revelations come through the imperfect bodies and minds of men touched by their Lord's perfection. Whenever a man dedicates his life to the service of his neighbors in the name and spirit of Christ the world beholds another, though minor, incarnation. Martin Luther put it even more strongly in his treatise On Christian Liberty. He said, "We ought freely to help our neighbors through our body and its works . . . that we may be Christs to one another." Our faith is neither this-worldly nor otherworldly. It is both spiritual and material. We show that we understand it only when we are willing to materialize in our activity and our life the spiritual meaning of our Lord.

[1] William Temple, Nature, Man, and God (New York: The Macmillan Co., 1949), p. 478.

XIX

TENSION AND PEACE

Think not that I came to send peace on the earth.
—Matt. 10:34
Peace I leave with you.   —John 14:27

A UNIVERSAL DESIRE IN OUR TIME IS TO BE RELIEVED OF THE ALMOST
unbearable tension under which we live. There have been few
times in the history of the world when a generation was so uncertain
of the future as ours. This uncertainty, added to the speed with
which we live, has produced in the lives of many men terrible
anxiety. As we have gone through periods of history labeled "the
age of enlightenment" and "the age of reason," so there is a sense
in which our time might very well be termed "the age of tension."

Many of us in recent days have been shocked by the passing of
friends in the prime of their lives. They were men who, to all outward appearance, had perfect health. Yet their untimely death
brought home to us that they had been the bearers of intolerable
burdens, and their life had been under an unendurable strain. There
are apparently few persons free from the problem of this strain. In
international relationships we talk about the war of nerves. Life to
many men has become a constant war of nerves, and the end is all
too apparent. They know it is only a question of time, unless
something happens to change the situation, until they will be
defeated in this struggle. If the gospel has anything to deal with
this crisis, now is the time to proclaim it. If men can find some way
to peace in the midst of the constant conflict, this would be the
best news our generation could hear.

202

The Enemy Is Anxiety

It has always been true that the great enemy of mankind is anxiety. It has probably destroyed more human life than any other enemy of the race. If at times it has not succeeded in killing a man, it has often so crippled him that he has become useless in the constructive efforts of life. Men are not made to be at high tension constantly. They need to find relief from it. It was said of an outstanding news commentator that if you touched him just before he went on the air, he would twang. Many a person, caught in the contemporary struggle and strain, has a nervous system so tense that no physical equipment can bear it.

All of this apparently has been the price we have had to pay for what we have called progress. A scientific generation that has developed tremendous speed has found that speed also entails a terrific cost. In our modern civilization too many successful men have experienced what we call, for want of a better name, a nervous breakdown. It is as if a kind of madness has taken hold of this generation, which demands that in the name of being social and business successes we must be failures as human beings. We are caught up in the midst of a competition that is so terrific we dare not pause for one moment lest we be chosen last. We live in a nightmare of being forced to take a place lower down.

As the years pass by, men caught in this trap dream of going back to the farm. Why did they leave it in the first place if this is what their final desire has come to be? If the competition of modern life can produce nothing finally except a desire to escape from it, is it too much to suggest that there is something wrong with our whole idea of success and our way of life? Many a man returns to the big city after a rest in a small town with a nostalgia for the quiet, calm, and peace of the simple life. Yet, as if he were hypnotized, he cannot escape from the prison he has entered. So he stumbles forward to the inevitable conclusion, which is a tired mind and a broken body.

Our civilization, rich in so many things, does not seem to have the power to produce calm and poise in people. There has never been a time so competent as ours in providing comforts and physical gadgets. Yet at the very hour when we have attained this victory we seem to have lost something which men must have if they are to live as men. One of the essentials has been left out. We come at last to the realization that it would be a good bargain if we could give up some of these things in order to attain a quietness of mind and a peace which religious men have known.

The situation has become so terrible that something must be done about it, and we know it. This is the reason thousands of people read a book on attaining peace of mind. Deep in their hearts they realize that the gift of the untroubled mind is the greatest gift God can bestow. Perhaps never before have so many people been aware of this truth as just now when they have lost their stability. There is a growing certainty upon us that there is no substitute for this inner quality of peace. We have tried to find exciting substitutes, and for the time being they seem to have worked. But as the miser cannot eat his gold, so these substitutes cannot feed our souls, nor bring us quietness.

Our generation would never admit a belief in evil spirits. Yet a vast number of our contemporaries live as if they were pursued by a host of devils. Life seems to be a losing race against impossible odds. There just are not enough resources for us to keep life steady and calm. We have the dreadful suspicion that we are living on our capital, and as far ahead as we can see there is no relief. The young hope that a few more changes will make life beautiful and meaningful. But at last there comes the certainty that it will not be different and we are doomed to a gradual spiritual deterioration.

It must never be assumed that tension is confined to the poor and the unsuccessful. Quite the opposite is the truth. The man with a family and an income that has to be stretched is too busy to worry about whether he is happy or not. But the people whose money gives them leisure and who are regarded by their neighbors as eminently successful are the ones who head for the psychiatrist. The strain is not caused by hard work but by empty achievements. It is not the woman whose family takes all her time who goes to pieces, but the idle woman who tires at last of thinking up amusements to help her through the vacant days. It is for such as these that a book was written with the satirical title *What to Do Until the Psychiatrist Comes.* As the New Testament says, "For we wrestle not against flesh and blood, but against principalities, against powers, against the rulers of the darkness of this world, against spiritual wickedness in high places." (Eph. 6:12 K.J.V.). But we are defeated because we lack the armor of God. The tragedy of the whole thing is that so many men continue to feverishly pursue that which, when attained, turns them into either invalids or neurotics.

The Unstrung Existence

Yet it must be said that there is no answer to this unbearable tension in simply retreating to an unstrung existence. One cannot withdraw from the demands of his life. One cannot say that he will take no responsibility for anything. One cannot withdraw from duty.

There is always the temptation to get used to things. We get too friendly with good fellows who shower us with favors and attention. Finally we can no longer be critical of these good friends, and the evil of their practices comes to be blurred in our minds. The sharpness of our judgment is dulled. This is failure. So the desire to take things just as they come and accept things just as they are is no solution to our tension. The problem will not go away by our simply pretending it is not there. There is no retreating to some pre-worry stage of life. We cannot go back again. There is no possible way for a man to recapture a childlike innocency and enter again into the delights of immaturity.

We are not going to reverse our civilization. We are not going to destroy our machines and go back to the simple agricultural experience of our forefathers. We are not going to make our living less complex simply because we are tired of it. There is no possible way we can take ourselves out of the stream of modern civilization. The trend is forward and not backward. The Utopian dream of a kind of society where no one works too much and no one worries because life has been simplified is a vain one, and we might as well forget it.

The truth is that to be human means to have tension. This is one of the prices we have to pay for being human. The subhuman life on the earth can know a peace which we cannot know. Facing men because they are men is the demand of duty and conscience. Challenging our ignoble desire for ease is the high call of noble sacrifice. Let no man be so foolish as to think that the solution of this problem of life is the elimination of all tension.

This has been attempted in our time, and the result has been almost worse than the tension which it sought to cure. Religion interpreted as comfort only is a great failure, for it is not really religion. Certainly the great Christian heresies of our time are represented by the sects which promise men Christianity without a cross. Only by casting a kind of spell over men's minds and making them drunk with words can one make them believe that life is a matter of imagining oneself into security. The silencing of the prophetic note is the stilling of God's voice.

The great appeal of these sects is due to the fact that we are in such desperate need of some kind of peace and comfort. We are wide open to the appeal of ease, and we will listen with intensity if someone can promise us relaxation from our worries. Those who follow these comfortable heresies sometimes obtain for themselves a kind of drugged content. It is to be noted, however, that we do not find social leadership or social criticism in these groups. They have been willing to replace the prophetic demand for reform with a selfish seeking of personal contentment. The established order need never fear such people, nor should the disinherited and the wronged ever expect any succor from them. When Christianity becomes a retreat, it is always a failure. Our religion is something that faces evil head on. It has never counseled choosing quietness of spirit at the expense of enlisting in moral battles. The unstrung life has never been the ideal held up by Jesus Christ. Too much of the religion of our time counsels getting rid of evil by imagining it is not there. It advises us to assume that if we ignore our trouble it will go away. Its priests induce a hypnotic effect by the use of soothing words and esoteric phrases. Listening to them is, in the words of John Rice describing the preaching of one of his relatives, like quietly getting drunk. But the situation demands something vastly more than this retreat.

A little boy was running swiftly down the street one day when he was stopped by a kindly old lady, who asked him, "My little boy, where were you going so fast?"

"I'm running for a doctor. My grandpa's sick."

"Now," said the lady, "you just run right back to grandpa and tell him he only thinks he's sick."

A couple of days later, the old lady saw the little boy again on the street, and she said to him, "How is your grandpa now?"

"Well," the boy replied, "he's all right now. He thinks he is dead, and we are going to bury him next Sunday." Let us understand that we are not going to solve our problems by assuming that there is no such thing as sickness or sorrow or dying. If there is to be an answer to the tensions of modern times, it will have to be in recognizing them and learning how to deal with them bravely and successfully.

FAITH

According to our religion, the answer to the problem is faith. In more ways than one men are saved by faith. A society is saved by faith, or it is destroyed by the lack of it. The tensions of life can be borne, even when they are as severe as they are in our time, if our faith is strong enough.

We need to believe that this is, after all, God's universe. For the Christian there is never the slightest doubt that the universe has been created by God in such a way that his word always has to be the last one. No Christian ever believes that things are out of hand and God is helpless. In a day when there hangs over the heads of mankind an atom bomb a great number of people have felt that praying to God is now useless. There seems to be the curious assumption on our part that not even God can do anything about an atom bomb. The Christian has the belief, to which he holds with tenacity, that if God Almighty made the atoms, God Almighty also made humanity, and his word is still the ultimate one.

Are things out of God's hands today? The answer to the Christian is obvious. They are never out of his hands, and nothing can ever happen to put them beyond his control. Is the death of a civilization an ultimate defeat for God? History says that this is not the case at all. Societies sometimes destroy themselves because they have not learned how to live according to the moral laws of life. Yet the end of a society is not the end of the human race, nor is it the end of the human experiment. Thus it is that in troubled times like ours the Christian is pessimistic about the immediate future, but he is utterly optimistic about the long future. It is not a comfortable thing to be caught in a dying society, but neither is it a matter of ultimate defeat for a man. We do not have to die; but if we cannot learn, and if we should die, still God is God, and the future is his.

Has our modern period suddenly put history into reverse? Are we a unique generation that has set loose forces that can defeat God? In spite of all the evil which men do, and in spite of all the barriers they raise against God's will, they cannot reverse the long plans of the Almighty. Our faith is that the universe conserves every good effort. We believe in the indestructibility of goodness. No sacrifice is ever in vain, and no brave act is ever annulled. Every minister learns the truth of this when he gets ready to leave his church. There come to him in those times men and women, young people and sometimes children, who tell him that at a particular time he said something or he did something that was helpful. He himself may have forgotten it long ago, and he may have never known there was anything connected with that particular statement or that act that had a redeeming quality in it. But he discovers that in every moment of his ministry, even when he was unaware of it, there was going out an unseen and powerful influence. Every man is like that. In the hour of our discouragement it is good to know that there are people we have helped and we knew it not. The good which men do lives after them, and long after they are gone the good act continues its triumphal march through the world.

A good life is never silenced, and virtue is never forgotten. Remember the ancient story of Cain and Abel in Genesis. After Cain has killed his brother and answered the Lord with the cynical question, "Am I my brother's keeper?" God replies to him, "The voice of thy brother's blood crieth unto me from the ground." It was the understanding of the Jew from the very beginning that there was nothing that could blot out the demand for justice from the ears of God. If it is true that no evil is ever forgotten and must always be punished, so it is also true that every good deed is eternal.

When Tolstoy, the great Russian novelist, was about fifty years old, he fell into a period of such deep depression that he seriously contemplated suicide. Everything had gone stale for him, and he wondered what the use of living really was. Then he tells us that the turning point came at a time when he was walking by himself in the woods. He thought of God, and the very thought brought welling up within his heart new courage and new joy. Suddenly it came to him that whenever he concentrated his mind on God, he had this experience of renewal and faith. And so he says that finally the realization came to him: "Why do I look further? He is there: he, without whom one cannot live. To acknowledge God and to live are one and the same thing. God is what life is. Well, then! Live; seek God. There will be no life without him!"

All of this means simply that the cure for the unbearable strain of tension and anxiety is faith in the living God. Let men who are engaged in an unsuccessful pursuit of happiness realize that until they come face to face with this truth, the pursuit is in vain and always must be. Tension is cured by faith.

PEACE OF TENSION

So it is that Jesus Christ brings to men a peace that seems to be a contradiction because it is associated with tension. Jesus was always offering men what seemed to them opposing things. He says, for example, that he came not to send peace but a sword. He talks about setting a man in defiance against his father and a daughter against her mother. He talks about a man's foes being those of his own household. He proclaims that if a man loves his father and mother more than he loves his Master, he is not worthy of him. He closes that passage with the wonderful paradox, "He that findeth his life shall lose it; and he that loseth his life for my sake shall find it." (Matt. 10:39.) It is almost as if Jesus were saying to us that two times two equals six. It is a denial of the laws of logic and reason. Men want the rewards of Christianity without being willing to face its stringent commands. But this is a fatal omission, and the result is a one-sided affair that is not Christian. They should learn that an attempt to divorce the promises of the gospel from its demands is an utter futility.

This teaching of Jesus presents no easygoing philosophy. How far removed it is from the saccharine lullabies of so much modern religion! There is in Jesus this sense of a deep and bitter enmity between himself and the world. There is no idea in his mind that the secular world will ever be anything but opposed to him and engaged in an endeavor to destroy him. He holds up before his followers the demand for a choice which involves sacrifice and suffering. As a matter of fact, the gospel itself comes upon men as a terrible tension, holding up before them life and death. The gospel is not peace but a sword. It is a frightening thing to many a man when he looks at it for the first time.

But over on the other side Jesus offers men peace, saying, "Peace I leave with you." (John 14:27.) Thus it is that the peace of Jesus Christ is the peace of tension and struggle and demand. It puts men at their best. In some strange way, as a man seeks to fulfill his obligations and do his duty for Christ's sake, there is given to him the calm and confidence which is the end of anxiety. The tension is no longer unbearable. A man feels high-strung now, spurred on to a great accomplishment, and in that very demand he has a contentment and a peace of mind which the unstrung worldling never knows. Thus it is that Christ comes to men, not to offer them contentment by removing the tension of life from them, but to bring them peace of mind by making the tension meaningful.

In 1939, when thousands of English children were evacuated from areas under aerial bombardment, the authorities thought they were doing the very best possible thing for those youngsters by making them physically safe. It was discovered, however, that children, especially if they were under five years of age, suffered emotional disturbances, though they were safe physically, because they had been removed from their parents' companionship and love. This is a clue for us. The thing which the children of God need most is not to be withdrawn from the bombardment of life and to be made physically safe. It is to come to know again the security that is ours in God, who surrounds us with his protection even in the very hour when the dangers of life are hardest to face. We discover that we who bear the strains of earthly life bear them not alone. At last we come to understand that the sword of Christ from which we have fled is also the peace of Christ for which we have longed.

XX

DEATH AND LIFE

> I have been crucified with Christ; . . . and that life which I now
> live in the flesh I live in faith.   —Gal. 2:20

ONE OF THE DECISIVE TESTS OF A WAY OF LIFE IS ITS ATTITUDE TOWARD
death. Death awaits every man, and a way of living which does not
have something humanly satisfying to say about it cannot long command the allegiance of mankind. A philosophy that counsels ignoring this fact and pretending that it does not exist can never be very
satisfactory for thoughtful people for any length of time. We
search for a positive word concerning the meaning of dying.

Whenever we lack faith, we seek cleverly to hide the fact of death.
George A. Buttrick writes:

When he does die, the undertaker strives to make it appear that he
has not died: he dresses him in a tuxedo, and lays him in a narrow box
as if he were asleep, even though a man does not usually sleep in a
tuxedo in a narrow box. There is a funeral, for, unfortunately for our
evasions, the man has died: "Too bad about So-and-so. But let's not
think about it!" So we run to our familiar hiding place in the sensate
world. And the cynic calls religion an "escape"! In truth, religion alone
refuses to be blind to the fact of death.[1]

The problem to be solved is not only one of fear. There are many
people who have no fear of death whatsoever. As a matter of fact,
the idea of death to many an individual caught in an impossible
situation, instead of being forbidding, is welcome. There are times
when men no longer desire to live and with the top of their minds

[1] *Christ and Man's Dilemma* (New York and Nashville: Abingdon-Cokesbury
Press, 1946), p. 85.

convince themselves that to die is desirable. When we observe a generation like ours plunging headlong into ultimate destruction and apparently controlled by an instinct which desires oblivion, we wonder if dying is not an easier way out than learning how to live. There are times in the history of the race when men are like the lemmings, migrating to the sea and death as if driven by forces beyond their control. Death seems to be what their beings most deeply desire. It is not, therefore, merely a philosophy to take away our fear of dying which we need, but an insight which can lift us above the defeat of death. Above everything else it is necessary that we look upon dying in such a way as to be unafraid of living. We need to learn how to live as if we would die tonight and work as if we would live forever.

It is the fear of life on the part of so many people which is the disturbing thing. It comes to us at last that there is some relationship between these seeming opposites. That is, until we can look at death victoriously, we are unable to live victoriously. The idea may be reversed also. We might say that until men learn to have victory over life, there is no possibility for them to have victory over death. Here are the great themes which we must ponder and about which we must reach some working conclusions.

If most of us should be asked to explain in a few sentences what we think about death and life, our probable answers would be complete silence. But down in the silent levels of our consciousness are certain great affirmations which we have accepted concerning both of these matters. They are the conclusions which determine the kind of persons we become, and they are the foundations of the faith by which we live. As William Ernest Hocking one time put it, "Man is the only animal that contemplates death, and also the only animal that shows any sign of doubt of its finality." [2] One of the greatnesses of the Christian faith is that it has a unique word to speak concerning the ultimate significance of death.

The Gospel writers have been criticized for spending so much time telling us the story of Jesus' death instead of telling us more

[2] *Thoughts on Death and Life* (New York: Harper & Bros., 1937), p. 5.

about his life. The thing which these critics do not see is that the death and life of Jesus are all of a piece. If his life sheds light on his death, then his death also sheds light on his life. In other words, the writers had the feeling that when they came to an understanding of the Crucifixion and the Resurrection, they had the essential clue to the Life. The sharp division which we moderns tend to make between a man's life and his death is meaningless and unreal to these Christian writers. They felt that the way a man dies gives the light we need in satisfactorily understanding his life.

To Kill the Body

For one thing, Christians have learned not to fear those who can only destroy the body. They remember the words of Jesus, "But rather fear him who is able to destroy both soul and body in hell." (Matt. 10:28.) Jesus taught that to assume the physical part of life is the primary part can only lead to defeat. "And Jesus answered him, saying, It is written, That man shall not live by bread alone, but by every word of God." (Luke 4:4 K.J.V.) Once a man has accepted the devil's assumption that the body is ultimate, all his values are completely reversed, and he no longer knows how to live intelligently. Let a man realize, as the Christian gospel insists, that he does not live on an earthly plane alone, and that because he is God's son, he is primarily a spirit. In the Christian scheme of things, therefore, the man who has power only over another man's body has power over something that is not of essential significance. It is when a man's spirit and mind are enslaved that an ultimate tragedy has occurred.

This is not debatable for the Christian, for he understands there is within him his real self, which has been granted a temporary use of the physical equipment. Our deepest concern, therefore, should not be what happens to us externally. These are matters which are important only so far as they have inner results. The ultimate defeat of any man's life is within his own heart. It is what happens to our thinking that is crucial. General Foch, referring to military strategy, remarked that a battle which is lost is one we

214

think is lost. This is why we are facing constantly the strange sight of two men going through the same experience which overwhelms the one and yet only makes the other stronger. Christians are those who do not fear men who have power over their bodies. They do not believe they are the victims of circumstances which have control over their physical environment.

William Law, who later wrote his *Serious Call to a Devout and Holy Life*, refused to take the oath of allegiance to King George I. That action cut off all chance of any advancement in the Established Church. He wrote to his brother at the time: "My prospect is melancholy enough, but had I done what was required of me to avoid it, I should have thought my condition much worse. The benefits of my education seem partly at an end, but that education had been miserably lost if I had not learned to fear something more than misfortune."

This is to say that no Christian ever subscribes to the philosophy of physical safety at any price. There are many things more important than security. Indeed, the Christian is very suspicious of material security, for he knows it produces not strength but weakness. His confidence lies in an inner power which has been given to him by God, and he never depends too much on the circumstances of his external environment.

It is this awareness that makes the gospel a constant obstacle to any victory of mere force. This is one of the strange things about Christians. They are not afraid of the things which their enemies think they should fear, and indeed they show an utter contempt for some forces which the pagan believes are all powerful. Once you are confronted by a group of people who no longer believe that what can be done to their bodies is of ultimate consequence, you are helpless in subjugating them and working your own will on them.

There is a story about Ivan the Terrible, who has been considered by many historians as the cruelest of the Russian czars. He was approached on the street one day by a ragged, barefoot monk called Teddy, who was much respected by the populace. The monk offered a piece of meat to the czar, who refused it, saying that it was Lent and he could not eat meat. "Ah," said the monk, "you do not eat meat, but you drink blood." The czar became enraged at this insult and would have destroyed the monk, but from the surrounding crowd there came the cry, "Czar, you may put us to death, but do not touch Teddy, because he is a man of God." Christians prefer to be numbered with men of God rather than with the tyrants who may have power to put them to death.

If men would only believe that they are merely bodies, they would believe they must at all costs protect those bodies. But precisely because this is not true, men will be loyal to things which mean their death. If men believe that it is better to live than die, no matter what their situation may be, everything is simplified, and they know exactly what to do. But this is the end of man's nobility and the destruction of his position as "a little lower than the angels."

What is the mighty power the Christian faith creates in men? It does not come to them as something overbearing or unjust. Never does it try to intimidate or bully them into heroism. It simply gives them a certainty that if their bodies are killed, no final disaster has overtaken them. There is about the gospel an urgency growing out of the atoning death of Christ which makes its demands impossible to escape. His preference for death over compromise is inescapable for his disciples. As Dr. Denny of Scotland one time put it, "To be a Christian, or not to be a Christian, is not a matter of comparative indifference; it is not the case of being a somewhat better man, or a man, perhaps, not quite so good; it is a case of life or death." It creates a loyalty that will ignore the threats of death.

It was this challenge which John Hampden gave to the burghers in the House of Commons. Said he: "To have printed liberties and not to have liberty in truth and realities is but to mock the kingdom. Shall it be treason to debase the king's coin though but a piece of sixpence and not treason to debase the spirits of his subjects, to set a stamp and character of servitude upon them?" It is this debasement of the spirit which the Christian sees as the ultimate tragedy. The stamp of servitude is more to be feared than the killing of the body.

Things Worse than Death

This means, of course, that for the Christian there are things worse than death. The democracies made the great mistake of assuming for a time that war was the worst possible thing that could happen. Once we have made that assumption, we have paved the way for those who are willing to use war as a means to achieve their goal. We have to realize that slavery and tyranny are worse things than war, and that rather than endure those worse things we will resist them. A policy of neutrality at any cost is futile and stupid. It overlooks the fact that neutrality is never possible for any man or nation, and that, whether we like it or not, we are always helping one side against the other. But even worse, it is an attempt to choose a selfish safety in preference to taking our place with the resisters of tyranny. So for a human being to assume that death is the worst possible thing means that he is already defeated. He is no longer a free person. But if he is willing to choose death rather than slavery, then he has been set free from the limitations of mortality.

Some of the older novels talked about the loss of virtue and chastity as a fate worse than death. The modern novelists tend to laugh at this kind of philosophy and assume that it is the product of a Mid-Victorian stuffiness. In a day when immorality does not seem to be very serious anyway and when promiscuity is assumed to be the general practice it would seem ridiculous to assume that any individual would prefer to die rather than be immoral. But I prefer to take my stand with the older novelists. At least it seems plain to me that those who follow a path of personal immorality come to a kind of death in life. This is the killing of the soul which is the eternal death. If our fathers sometimes made the choice a little too simple and a little too sentimental, they nevertheless had a true understanding of reality. When man has bartered his purity for the sake of physical thrills, he has lost sight of what is primary and final.

Betrayal is always worse than defeat. Whenever a man betrays his best for the sake of a worldly success, he enters into a state that is best described as a living death. Sooner or later such men come to have a very deep envy for the man who has dared, amid the difficulties of this life, to surrender success for the sake of his integrity. If the truth were known, our world is full of men who would gladly trade their Dun and Bradstreet rating for a clear conscience and peace of mind. A more serious prostitution than selling one's body is selling one's self-respect, though it may be legal. What is more tragic than the "tired liberals" who have traded their birthrights for profit? There is no greater sign of Jesus' realism than his warning that when a man has lost his soul, he has lost everything.

The betrayal of a friend is worse than death. Whenever any man fails in his personal relationships and has chosen to sacrifice a human being for his own selfish benefit, he has made one of those evil bargains which corrupts every chance he might have had for happiness. For when we have sold out our devotion and our loyalty, we have betrayed one of the essential claims of our humanity. To betray a cause is to lay up for ourselves an everlasting shame. Our own little lives do not count for too much in physical terms, no matter how important we may think we are. But the great causes for which we can stand and for which we can be symbols make us as giants in the earth. To prefer an ignoble safety over a danger to be risked for a noble cause is a failure which will haunt every quiet moment. Until restitution has been made for our betrayal, we live like murderers.

Whenever we are content to deny truth for the sake of the lie, we have made a bargain which is, in many ways, worse than dying. Or when we have failed to do our duty, we cannot live with ourselves until we have repented. The truth is that if we are realistic about human experience, many things in life are worse than dying. There are realms in which our failure is not just ephemeral but eternal.

The fiery sermons of the eighteenth-century American preacher Jonathan Edwards are too extreme for our modern ears. There is a ruthlessness in his theology we cannot believe is always Christian. We shudder when we read something like the following section from one of his sermons:

When the saints in glory, therefore, shall see the doleful state of the damned, . . . when they shall see the smoke of their torment, and the raging of the flames of their burning, and hear their dolorous shrieks and cries, and consider that they in the meantime are in the most blissful state, and shall surely be in it to all eternity; how will they rejoice! . . . How joyfully will they sing to God and the Lamb, when they behold this.

But there is one essential thing Jonathan Edwards had which we have lost. He understood that it is not the dying that is the significant thing, but it is the kind of destiny we have created for ourselves by our living. The Christian is one who has learned to lose his fear of those who can only affect him materially. For he knows that there are many worse things than the passing experience of death.

Quality and Not Quantity

For the Christian life is a matter of quality and not quantity. He is not particularly concerned about the number of years, but he is terribly concerned about the kind of years he lives. A scientific generation has assumed that the greatest boon it could give mankind was to stretch out the life span. We have been very proud of our ability to make life longer. Yet if at the same time we make its quality less instead of increasing that too, our achievement is a very questionable one.

When we study history and consider our contemporaries, we are aware that great men often live so short a time. It is very difficult for a man to have any great envy for the person who has had mere length of years. We know from our own experiences that we sometimes live more in two minutes than we have lived at other times in two months. We know also that often, if the choice were up to us, we would be glad to trade a number of days for one great moment which we remember.

What is a truly tragic funeral? Is it a funeral where death has come suddenly to someone in the midst of life and health? Is it necessarily the death of a child who has gone before he has had his chance to live? Is it sudden death of any kind? More and more it seems to me that the most tragic funeral a minister has to conduct is for the individual who has never really lived. When a man dies without leaving behind him friends, that is tragic. When a man dies without ever having contributed to the world, that is disaster. When a man dies without having created within his own spirit something that is worthy of paradise, then that is ultimate failure. A man's life does not consist of the things he possesses nor of the abundance of years he may have enjoyed.

The truth is that the termination date of the Christian's life is not of primary importance at all. Since we do not believe we come to an end but go on, it is not too significant whether the crossing takes place now or ten years from now. The Christian, therefore, is much more concerned that he should use his days wisely than that he should preserve as many of them as possible. As Paul one time put it, we sometimes feel a kind of longing for the time of our departure and the moment when our spirits shall be called home. Yet that experience does not minimize the meaning of our present life but only succeeds in giving the present even more significance and meaning. When men can look at death like that, the primary question is not when death shall come but only how we shall live to make life here worthy of eternity.

The desire to hoard is taken away from the Christian, for as George MacDonald puts it:

The heart of man cannot hoard. His brain or his hand may gather into its box and hoard, but the moment the thing is passed into the box, the heart has lost it and is hungry again. If a man would have, it is the Giver he must have. . . . Therefore all that he makes must be free to come and go through the heart of his child; he can enjoy it only as it passes, can enjoy only its life, its soul, its vision, its meaning, not itself.

All of this means that the Christian experience interprets quality and not quantity.

Never far from the Christian's thought is the assurance that he has forever. The death of a civilization is a final defeat neither for

God nor for a Christian. Since our souls are the ultimate things about us, we already dwell in eternity, and the change from life to death is not nearly so abrupt as men without faith think. Our life is lived in faith, as Paul said. For having in some strange way gone through the experience of being crucified with Christ, we now have the great assurance that we are also raised from the dead by him and with him. We come to know at last that without the death experience we could not know life. Until we too have shown our ability to triumph over the material powers of life, we cannot enter into the life eternal.

This experience of eternal life, now, comes to the Christian, bringing with it a great patience and a great calm. With eternity having already broken in upon him through his relationship with Christ, he lives in a world where the victory of death has been canceled and the sting of death has been destroyed. With the glad confidence that at last we have become "more than conquerors through him that loved us" our life can now become a matter of triumph and assurance.

Archaeologists unearthing ancient Roman cemeteries found an inscription on tombstones which occurred so often that sometimes just the first letters of the word were used. It said, "I was not; I was; I am not; I do not care." There may be a certain stoical courage shown here, but there is nothing to inspire men or transform them. Contrast with that John Brown's word in Edwin Arlington Robinson's dramatic monologue: "I shall have more to say when I am dead." Is death for us to be a great nothingness? Is it to be only a great silence? Not so. In the experience of our risen Lord we find a kind of life that conquers dying. Our life here is lived in faith, and our death will be but another victory of our faith.

Carl Van Doren's fine book on the Constitutional Convention and the writing of the American Constitution is entitled significantly The Great Rehearsal. He says that the American experience and accomplishment must be regarded as a rehearsal in miniature of what the world must now do. As a number of colonies became a nation, now a number of nations must become one world. So in

Paul's thought the Christian experience in this life is a rehearsal for his eternal career after death. We have been crucified to sin and raised from that death by Christ. Now our life is a matter of faith, and our death will be an experience we have already rehearsed. That future death and resurrection will no doubt be greater than anything we have known, but it will not be entirely strange to us. In our Christian faith we live and die and shall live again.

XXI

ALL THE FULLNESS

And he is before all things, and in him all things consist.
—Col. 1:17

WHENEVER WE STUDY THE MEANINGS OF THE CHRISTIAN FAITH, IT takes us only a short time to get beyond our depth. Its breadth, height, and depth are beyond our reach. Only little minds unaware of their littleness are willing to say some silly thing like, "Christianity is just a practice of the Golden Rule." When we are caught in its splendor, we never assume we can ever come close to a full comprehension of our faith. When the gospel found a great mind like the apostle Paul's, it at once struck a responsive note. For with his spiritual sensitivity and his long search for what he had not found he was able to appreciate something as great as Jesus Christ. Out of the few brief letters which come down to us from his hand—and the authorship of some of those, of course, has been disputed—the Christian Church has found enough ideas to keep its greatest minds busy for nineteen centuries. The profundities in the apparent simplicities of Jesus led the author of the Epistle to the Colossians to say that we should all walk worthily of our heritage, and we should give thanks to God who, "translated us into the kingdom of the Son of his love; in whom we have our redemption, the forgiveness of our sins: who is the image of the invisible God, the firstborn of all creation; for in him were all things created, in the heavens and upon the earth, things visible and things invisible, whether thrones or dominions or principalities or powers; all things have been created through him, and unto him; and he is before all things, and in him all things consist." (1:13-17.) Here is an affirmation that the seeming contradictions of life find their harmony and balance in Jesus. Here is the insistence that in our Lord we can find the unity for which we search.

It is the gospel's understanding of truth that it must be revealed in personal terms. It is the gospel's understanding of morality that it has to be seen in action. There are things which come not by reason but by revelation through a life. For Christians the mysteries are revealed in the life, the teaching, the death, and the resurrection of Christ. In him there dwells all the fullness, and looking unto him we see the solution of the paradoxes.

GOD DESIRES FELLOWSHIP

Religion begins with the assumption that God desires fellowship with his children. This is another one of its marked differences from philosophy. The philosopher assumes that God remains aloof, entirely unconcerned as to whether we understand him or not. To find him is altogether our task and our responsibility. God has to be discovered by our reason. He is an unmoved mover. This is quite different from the religious man's experience. For him there comes the realization that we are found by God. It is God who takes the initiative. No man is so desperately concerned over this matter of our fellowship with him as he is. The religious man sees his presence at every turning and hears his voice in every whisper of his own conscience. He is convinced in his heart that his seeking of God is possible only because he has already been found by God.

One of the serious mistakes in modern times has been a denial of this truth. We have tried to build a religion around the idea of a passive Deity. There follows from this idea the assumption that religion is entirely dependent upon human willingness to search and human ability to understand. It is because of this heresy that we have come to think of God as almost anything that is virtuous, and we have come to regard religion as almost anything that partakes of the nature of altruism. It is the kind of religion accepted by an irreligious generation. It will not stand the test of crisis. Times of danger demand a theology and not a philosophy.

This is not to say that human effort is unnecessary. It is not to say that mankind is helpless to do anything for his own salvation. It is not to say that God is "wholly other." But it is to say that if we are to enter into the joy of the sons of God, our first necessity is to know that before we were aware of our need he was reaching out to us. The curious thing is that the more we are aware that it is God who acts first, the more our human efforts are inspired and achieve results. It is like the child who buys his father a present out of his allowance. Such a generous act is pleasing to the parent, and it reveals a generous and loving spirit. It is very meet, right, and proper for the child so to do. But it is also his bounden duty, and if anyone assumes that because of that transaction the father is more wealthy by the price of the gift, he is simply thinking nonsense. So the man who has the idea he can do something for his heavenly Father is really thinking nonsense too. Of course there is a sense in which we can do something for God by showing him our appreciation and our love. But as the religious geniuses have all understood, everything we can do for him is only proper and no more than he has a perfect right to expect. This is why Christians come to revel in the grace of God which reveals itself most clearly in his willing-ness to seek us until we are found.

The love of God is revealed to us in this process. Like all love, it is positive and takes the initiative. It does not wait. It offers itself long before it is deserved and long before men can even dimly comprehend its significance. It will never acknowledge defeat but will wait until the time comes when it can lead us into an awareness of its presence. One of the chief implications of Jesus' teaching concerning the fatherhood of God is the assumption that he has time to hear our calls and waits for the time when we will turn to him. God's patience is a judgment on our impatience and lack of faith. As the psalmist said: "When my father and my mother for-sake me, then the Lord will take me up." (Ps. 27:10.) He has time for all his children, and he practices a persistent seeking that is enough to break down our pride and destroy our sin.

There is a story about Mendelssohn that one of his pupils used to get him up in the morning by playing loudly an unresolved chord. The great master could not stand it, and in spite of his desire to stay in bed, he had to jump up and run downstairs and resolve that chord. So when human life is unable to produce the harmony of which it is truly capable, God apparently cannot stand it but must come to the rescue. He desires fellowship with us, and he seeks it. Human inadequacy draws on God's sympathy with irresistible force. He is like the father of the prodigal son.

Once again let us look at our human situation and assume that God is at least as good as men. There may be some parents who will go no further toward helping their children than the law demands. At least you read about them in the paper from time to time. But they do not represent the norm. As a matter of fact the general public is shocked by such disclosures and feels a vague kind of shame as if the whole race had been disgraced. Most parents have grown so sensitive to the needs of their children that they stand ready to answer before they are called. Parents go seeking lost children before the children know they are lost. Paul described God's seeking of his lost children thus: "But God commendeth his own love toward us, in that, while we were yet sinners, Christ died for us." (Rom. 5:8.)

OBSTACLES

But there are certain great obstacles which stand in the way of this divine activity. It is all right to talk glibly about man's having fellowship with God. But it is not so easy to talk about when one begins to comprehend all the significance of it. There is, for one thing, God's own nature which seems to stand as a great obstacle to man's fellowship with him. The holiness of God was one of the great doctrines which the prophets always insisted upon and which every religious teacher has visioned. How can the holiness of God in any way have fellowship with the evil of human beings? His way

226

is not our way, and the very suggestion that God would in any way forget his holiness or forget his hatred of evil in order to commune with men is in itself obviously untenable.

Nor will the Almighty override a man's own personal freedom and insist on fellowship whether a man wants it or not. He will wait until it is given to him freely and honestly. He must wait until the blindness is gone from a man's eyes, and the hardness has been dissolved from his spirit. It demands more patience to pave the way for the vision of God than anyone except God would have. One sees something of this process in the great father or in the great teacher. How terrible is the inability of the child to understand the revelation of the father's love or the revelation of the teacher's truth! What patience it demands and what persistence it takes to bring the process to a successful conclusion!

Over against this stumbling block of the holiness of God is the stumbling block of man's sin. There is man's stubborn pride which refuses to recognize his need for help until it is, humanly speaking, too late. There is his blindness which moves amid spiritual truth and sees it not. There is his twisted spirit which has lost the power to comprehend the most elementary spiritual reality. There is his deafness which does not hear the still small voice. There is his failure to learn by experience and thus be led to repentance and redemption.

Chancellor von Bethmann-Hollweg made a speech to the German Reichstag in 1914. He said: "Gentlemen, we are now in a state of necessity, and necessity knows no law! Our troops have occupied Luxemburg, perhaps even have already entered Belgian territory. Gentlemen, this violates rules of international law. . . . The injustice—I speak frankly—the injustice which we thus commit we will try to make good again as soon as our military goal has been achieved." Here is the obstacle which stands in the way of man's communing with God. It is the failure to comprehend the moral law and the inability of any man to achieve his purpose by ignoring it. Blind stubbornness, deafness, evil, sin—all of these raise the barriers in the way.

227

THE PARTIAL REVELATIONS

It is no wonder, therefore, that the things which reveal God can do so only partially. Nature can reveal to us something that is meaningful. There are times when it has the power to stir us in a strange way. Almost every person who has not grown entirely insensitive to beauty has had the experience of feeling an emotional lift in the presence of some awe-inspiring scene. But a man can look in vain into the secrets of nature to find any saving kind of revelation for himself. The answer to human sin and human tragedy is not apparent in the mountains or in the sea.

Today when men wish to play golf or picnic on the Sabbath, they claim that men can worship just as well outside the church as they can inside it. But the trees, the brooks, and the flowers, while they may bring us a certain calmness and relaxation, do not bring us an answer to the terrible question of why a man must suffer innocently. The religion of nature has much about it that is commendable. All men who live in cities will find their raveled sleeves of care, anxiety, and weariness bound up by experiences in the country. But men seeking answers to the questions of their personal existence do not find it in nature. The god of nature is too easily lost in nature's processes and then identified with them. We do feel a presence of something in far vistas which is more than human. But we cannot say that in that view God is reconciling the world to himself. After all has been said and done, the revelation of God in nature, while a very precious thing, is only a partial thing so far as his relation to the human situation is concerned.

Another of the partial revelations is human reason. We will be quite wrong if we despise reason, as some religious groups do. We will be quite wrong if we try to minimize what reason can do. It can lead us a long way, and indeed anything that is contrary to reason is no revelation at all. Reason teaches us to believe in a Creator. Reason saves us from being content with the illogical interpretations of experience. Every man who thinks very profoundly for any length of time is driven at last to search for an intelligent purpose

228

to live by. The value of what our fathers called "natural theology" is not to be despised.

But the very idea of reason is a limiting one. It is limited by human life and human experience. If reason is all, then we must assume that anything beyond our own minds is impossible for us to understand or experience. In the vast mysterious realm of life reason cannot satisfy us. The limitless ocean of the unknowable is so great that we are cut off from ever feeling at home here if we must stop at the edge of it. But it is this great mystery which brings men finally to their knees in a prayer for something which they cannot comprehend or ever reach with their minds. It is like the Breton fishermen's familiar prayer: "Protect us, Father. Our ship is so small; thy sea is so vast." Yet that prayer also reveals an experience which goes far beyond reason. It is an experience which could reach out and say, "Father." It is an acquaintance and fellowship with Someone in the universe whose mystery has somehow been dimly comprehended by the human heart.

The law as a revelation of God is not to be minimized. One of the greatest possessions of men is the Judaic law which to the believer is a revelation of God. To understand the moral behavior of life and the necessity of moral responsibility is one of the most significant steps forward man has made. That men could come to have a real affection for the law and learn to say, "I love thy law," was in itself something before which we can bow.

Yet Paul's experience with the law was not a satisfying one. It was something which condemned him and made inner peace impossible of attainment. It created, in his life at least, an impossible tension. It revealed a human need that was too great to ever be fulfilled by human effort alone. It was, as Clement of Alexandria said, a kind of tutor which led a child to the teacher. It was a forerunner, and it proclaimed a moral order and a moral demand which human life could not ignore. But it did not, and in fact it could not, reveal the one thing a man needed to find, namely, power adequate for his salvation.

We cannot ignore the fact that a great number of people have found the law to be satisfying, and they have regarded the Christian interpretation of it as a misleading exaggeration. That the ordinary worshiper would ever react to the law as Paul did was not to be expected. But his insight points up one inescapable truth, that if God is a person, then it takes more than legalities, no matter how just and merciful they may be, to reveal his nature to men. Even orthodox Judaism had something of this feeling, as is shown by its tendency to personalize the law.

Human experiences teach us a good deal, and God certainly uses our experiences to reveal himself. The difficulty, however, is that we do not learn enough from them. We need only to look at history to realize that the nations and the generations go on making the same blunders time after weary time. What is true in this larger setting is also true of individuals. Apparently we are not as bright as we ought to be when it comes to learning from our experience. We need something to tell us what that experience means and interpret it in such a way that it can become for us a lamp unto our feet.

Thomas Merton writes from his monastery: "For until we love God perfectly His world is full of contradictions. The things He has created attract us to Him and yet keep us away from Him. They draw us or they stop us dead. We find Him in them to some extent and then we don't find Him in them at all." [1] So in all these partial revelations of God there is that which attracts us up to a point, but there is not that which enables us to speak to God as a man speaks with his friend or to love him and hear his saving word.

God Was in Christ

It is the Christian experience that this deep need is fulfilled at last in Jesus Christ. God was in Christ. This is the very center of our faith and the unique part of our Christian experience. Through Jesus Christ men come to have more than a nodding acquaintance with God. In him is all God's fullness and all God's loving concern.

[1] *Seeds of Contemplation* (Norfolk: New Directions, 1949), p. 22.

In Jesus, God speaks with words which penetrate into our understanding.

There are too many people, and some of them are Christians, who assume that Jesus is to be thought of primarily as an idealist and a dreamer. They think of him as one who said some very beautiful and lovely things about life. They put him in the same category as the poet who writes about life with a touching tenderness. They take him with the same seriousness salesmen take pep talks. Their attitude toward him is often one of condescension and superiority. Oh yes, they assume it was sweet of him to be the way he was. But of course, their attitude seems to say, when a man gets out into the practical things of life, he learns he cannot take Jesus' commands too seriously.

The thing men have to learn is that Jesus said these things, not because they are nice, not because they are sweet, but because they are true. Until we come to understand the realism of Jesus Christ, we will never comprehend his divine office. In his commands we have the word which will bring us into right relationship with reality. In his insights we have a vision of the way things actually are. Jesus shows us what God is.

It is this central and unique thing about our gospel that we can so easily neglect and forget. Christians, in the name of sophistication, leave out this most significant part of it all. They forget that the clue to the whole mystery of God is in our affirmation that God is like Jesus Christ. The concern which he had for the disinherited is the concern which God has for men. All his sympathy for the downtrodden is God's sympathy for us. All his willingness to suffer and die is the willingness of God to endure sacrificial suffering that we might be saved. Here is the complete revelation that brings us to our knees. Here is the experience which opens our eyes and unstops our ears. Here is all the satisfying fullness of the love of God for men. In Christ we see the goodness and severity, the mercy and the judgment, the wisdom and the foolishness of God.

So at last we see that in the wisdom of God it took a human

231

life to resolve the paradoxes of life. What nothing else was able to do Jesus Christ could do and did do. Men do not understand these mysteries until they see them actually clarified in a person. If God is personal and we are human, then we would have to assume that sooner or later he would find his way into our hearts through a person. This is exactly what the Christian faith says has happened in Christ.

The tensions and strains of human experience are not solvable in any academic way. There is a sense in which the more we talk about them the more impossible it is to ever understand them. The laws of reason are helpful until we enter that mysterious realm where reason cannot go. Human experience is a valuable guide until a man has experienced something that cannot be defined. In vain the man who has seen the unseeable endeavors to describe it for the others. His words will not give us the import of the meaning of his vision. It is all very well to advise men to be calm like the mountains, steadfast like the sea, and fixed like the stars. But we are not mountain nor sea nor star. We are men living in the personal realm and utterly incapable of receiving an adequate revelation from the impersonal.

Like every great experience, this coming to God by the pathway of Christ has been bitterly debated and angrily argued. So much of the theological controversy of the past centuries has centered around defining the person of Christ. Was he God or man or both? But after we have exhausted our mental powers, we know that precise statement is impossible. To make Jesus a deity robs his humanity of any meaning and makes the example of his life a farce. To make him only a good man contradicts the salvation which men find in him and find nowhere else. We will do well to be content with Paul's word that God was in Christ. It will be best to rest on the Christian assurance that when we have seen Jesus, we have seen a vision of God. Let us rejoice that God "hath in these last days spoken unto us by his Son." In him the one who made the lion and the lamb to dwell together comes to set us free from the tensions and conflicts of our humanity. After we have practiced our excesses long enough and followed the fads far enough, at last we come back to the sanity and the harmony of Jesus Christ.

When Bertrand Russell was asked, "Do you fully understand the Einstein theory of relativity? Do you go with him all the way?" he replied, "I answer the first question in the negative and the second in the affirmative." This is what the Christian's faith in Jesus Christ means. Do we understand him completely! No! Can we set the boundaries about his personality? No! Is there any theological statement which entirely describes the person and work of Christ? There is none. But can we accept him as the perfect revelation of God and the truth about men and their destiny? Yes! Can we find salvation by accepting his lordship over our lives? Yes, and, like our fathers before us, we do. Or as Colossians puts it, "For it was the good pleasure of the Father that in him should all the fullness dwell." (1:19.)

Some time ago a talented young writer and editor bought a country newspaper in New England. With exceptional literary power and discernment he wrote about the ordinary happenings in the little village. But he wrote about them in such a way that one man said, "Your items are so local they're universal." Something like that is our experience with Jesus. He was a man who lived in a particular time and in a particular situation. He was a man as we are men, and at the same time he was used of God to make his universal love plain to us. When we have seen him, we know that we have found "the wild truth reeling but erect." The Christian adventure has been to drive forward between the tame relaxation of heresy and the siren call of oversimplification. It is by the gospel's power to make the lion and the lamb dwell together as they did in Jesus that we are saved.